77 Billion to One:

2016 Election Fraud

An Analysis of Altered Primary Exit Polls, Rigged Voting Machines, Uncounted Ballots, Cumulative Vote Shares, DNC Emails, Adjusted Pre-election Presidential Polls and Media Disinformation

Richard Charnin

Previous books by Richard Charnin

Matrix of Deceit: Forcing Pre-election and Exit Polls to Match Fraudulent Vote Counts
Richard Charnin is an expert in this field, the real deal, and, to put it simply, he proves amazing things with numbers. He does amazing things with the data, and it isn't magic, it's Math! GREAT book! There couldn't be more important work at a more important time than this analysis of our voting process. There is no process more integral and vital to our democracy -- and the integrity of the process should not be negotiable. Richard Charnin's simple math PROVES that our electoral process requires immediate attention.
- David Wayne, co-author with Richard Belzer of the New York Times Bestseller "Dead Wrong"

Proving Election Fraud: Phantom Voters, Uncounted Votes and the National Poll
Richard Charnin used to do the math necessary for the design of space craft and advanced fighters. Here he turns his professional skills to election fraud that consistently produces election results at great variances from both the "true vote" count and the vote count indicated by voters surveyed in scientific exit polls.
- Cliff Arnebeck, Election Attorney, Columbus, Ohio

Reclaiming Science: The JFK Conspiracy
Reclaiming Science: The JFK Conspiracy features an apt title because it entails reclaiming the legitimate content that has hitherto been obfuscated and distorted under the specious science (or what I call pseudo-science) of the Warren Commission Report. Granted, it likely won't be on any NY Times best sellers' lists but I found it to be one of the best new books on the JFK assassination to emerge in the past 25 years. Charnin, a former consultant and quantitative programmer for investment banks, has written a mathematical masterpiece which uses Poisson analysis to show a significant number of witness deaths in the wake of the JFK assassination were indeed unnatural. **- Philip A. Stahl, PhD Physics**

77 Billion to One

Table of Contents

Introduction

The 2016 Democratic primaries have finally awakened the public to Election Fraud. Millions of voters who were unaware or in denial came to realize that our election system was rigged and that the mainstream media is complicit in covering up Election Fraud.

The media and its cadre of exit poll naysayers in the corporate media don't dare mention the third-rail of American politics – election fraud. The media pundits remain silent on electronic vote rigging. They maintain that the exit polls are inaccurate and call truth-seeking activists conspiracy buffs.

The media is silent on the 2015 Year in Elections report, an independent research project by 2,000 elections experts from Harvard University and the University of Sydney. The report ranked the United States dead last in electoral integrity among established Western democracies in evaluating the integrity of 180 national parliamentary and presidential contests held July 1, 2012 to December 31, 2015 in 139 countries worldwide.

This book focuses largely on exit polls since they are the focus of virtually all naysayer arguments. But cumulative vote share analysis is based on actual vote counts and is a companion method. The two mathematical methods confirm each other and overwhelmingly prove election fraud. The State Department relies on exit polls in elections overseas to check for fraud if the discrepancies exceed 2%. There is no such check in the U.S.

Overwhelming evidence shows that Sanders won the primaries, despite the 3 million Clinton vote margin repeated endlessly in the media. He won the vast majority of 18-34 year-old voters. His positions on Wall Street corruption, universal health care, eliminating student debt, etc. made him an overwhelming favorite among young voters.

Sanders won the caucuses with an average 65% share. Exit polls indicated that he did at least 4% better than recorded vote, reducing Clinton's margin is reduced from 3 to 1 million. But it is a documented fact that millions of Sanders' voters were disenfranchised by stripping voter rolls and uncounted provisional ballots. Voter rolls were hacked in support of Clinton. Voting machines and central tabulators are manufactured by right wing corporations. No one can view the proprietary software. Machine vote flipping is just part of the story.

There were scores of documented cases of voter suppression. In California thousands who were registered to vote at the polls discovered that they were registered as mail-ins. They were given provisional ballots, many of which were trashed and never counted.

The number of polling places were reduced. Long lines and waiting times of over four hours benefited the candidate who had the most mail-in votes. Arizona was called for Clinton before the polling stations closed.

Sanders's exit poll share exceeded his recorded share by more than the margin of error in at least 11 of 26 primaries- a one in 77 billion probability. He won the vast majority of rural counties, but lost in urban areas where the votes were stolen. The difference in vote share was counter-intuitive; the progressive candidate always does better in urban and suburban areas.

The National Election Pool consists of six media giants and fund exit pollster Edison Research. In the six presidential elections from 1988-2008, the Democrats led the 274 unadjusted exit polls by an average of 52-42%, but won the recorded vote by just 48-46%. In addition, 232 of the 274 polls red-shifted to the Republican in the vote and 135 exceeded the margin of error- 131 for the Democrats. The probability is zero.

1. Recent Developments

Hillary Clinton and her supporters in the media claim that an "October Surprise" from Russia will influence the election. But election fraud is home-grown. We have entered the Twilight Zone.

The *Wikileaks* emails proved that the DNC supported Clinton and "rigged" the election. After ignoring and attacking election analysts since 2000, the corporate media and the Clinton campaign are finally warning of presidential election fraud - by the Russians!

The Democratic Party has moved to the right in seeking to maintain the status quo. Clinton and her supporters in the media claim that an "October Surprise" from Russia will influence the election. But election fraud is home-grown. They promote the fiction that that Russia could rig the elections but cover up the massive historical evidence of U.S. Election Fraud! The Democrats and Clinton demonize Putin, claiming he will rig the election for Trump. This is pure propaganda.

Clinton and Trump are the two most unpopular candidates in history. Both have approval ratings near 40%.

Trump stated that the election will be rigged based on the 2016 primaries. He notes that the primaries were stolen from Sanders but does not refer to the rigged voting machines in his focus on the Wikipedia DNC leaks. Voter suppression has always been a Republican tactic. Trump and the corporate media have ignored the historical "red shift" of votes to the GOP.

Third-party candidates Jill Stein and Gary Johnson have major support in the 18-34 age group. Clinton is viewed as dishonest and untrustworthy by a majority of these voters.

Stein has attracted young voters who were overwhelmingly for Sanders. She is for pardoning whistle-blowers and switching to cleaner energy sources and opposed to foreign wars and regime change. Millennials want to focus on domestic economic, political, and social problems.

Roger Stone is a long-time Republican operative from the Nixon era. Stone wrote in *The Hill*: *"Can the 2016 Elections Be Rigged? You Bet"* in which he referred to my posts on Wisconsin election fraud and *"The Strip & Flip Selection of 2016: Five Jim Crows & Electronic Election Theft"* by Bob Fitrakis and Harvey Wasserman.

A recent study by Stanford University proved that Hillary Clinton's campaign rigged the system to steal the nomination from Bernie Sanders. What was done to Bernie Sanders in Wisconsin is stunning. Why would the Clintons not cheat again?

The issue here is both voter fraud, which is limited but does happen, and election theft through the manipulation of the computerized voting machines, particularly the DIEBOLD/PES voting machines in wide usage in most states.

POLITICO profiled a Princeton professor — who has demonstrated how the electronic voting machines that are most widely used can be hacked in five minutes or less! Robert Fitrakis Professor of Political Science in the Social and Behavioral Sciences Department at Columbus State Community College has written a must-read book on the strip and flip technique used to rig these machines. Professor Fitrakis is a Green Party activist.

A computer hacker showed CBS how to vote multiple times using a simple $15.00 electronic device.

Mathematician and voting statistic expert Richard Charnin has produced a compelling study by comparing polling to actual results and exit polls to make a compelling case for voting machine manipulation in the Badger state.

Corporate Media Finally Admits the Obvious

In an article posted on July 28, 2016, NBC News pointed out that our elections are vulnerable to hacking because they "*are not part of the vast 'critical infrastructure protection' safety net set up by the Department of Homeland Security.*" But the threat to our election system comes from private for-profit corporations, control voter databases, count the votes using secret proprietary software. There is no transparency.

CBS News on August 10, 2016, mentioned "*the hackers at Symantec Security Response*" who demonstrated how "*Election Day results could be manipulated by an affordable device you can find online.*"

The Washington Post wrote: "*Deleting or altering data on voter rolls could cause mayhem on Election Day disenfranchising some voters. Many voting machines themselves also are vulnerable, especially touch-screen systems that do not create a paper record as a guard against fraud or manipulation.*" The Post also supplied a list of the 15 states with the most vulnerable voting systems.

The list of those now admitting the obvious includes the Boston Globe, The Atlantic, USA Today, The Guardian, Mother Jones, and Politico and The Hill, which warned that hackers could target voter records. "*A series of data breaches overseas are spurring concerns that hackers could manipulate elections in the United States.*"

Racketeering Lawsuit

A major lawsuit has been filed by the Institute for American Democracy and Election Integrity. The group noted the significant difference between the exit polls and the vote totals shifting from Bernie Sanders to Hillary Clinton as statistically impossible.

Cliff Arnebeck has been preparing a RICO lawsuit . Arnebeck got his J.D. from Harvard. He is the chair of the Legal Affairs Committee of Common Cause Ohio and a national co-chair and attorney for the Alliance of Democracy. His co-counsel, Bob Fitrakis, is an election lawyer and political science professor.

Computer security expert Stephen Spoonamore has worked with Arnebeck on exposing GOP election fraud in Ohio. He notes that when exit poll data varies more than 2% from electronic vote totals, the totals are questionable. In fact, 2% is the criteria the US State Dept, uses to determine if elections in foreign nations are fraudulent. **Exit poll differences in the 2016 DNC primaries listed above are** significantly greater than 2%. These differences point to questionable results for the electronic vote totals and likely electronic vote switching.

The Institute for American Democracy and Election Integrity (ADE), the Columbus Institute of Contemporary Journalism, and Democracy Counts set up exit polls and audits to track apparent election results in California.

Various lawsuits are in progress. Bob Fitrakis has filed suit to get raw, precinct-level exit polls from Edison. Chicago's board of elections was sued to redo the voting machine audit. In San Diego, election officials are being sued for excluding certain ballots from a random audit.

Election Justice USA

A report by EJUSA, a nonprofit election integrity organization is recommending that Democratic primary results in numerous states, including New York and California, be decertified and that the paper ballots be recounted by hand in all states which show irregularities, where paper ballots are available, and counted by hand in all future US elections. Certification of election results is from the Secretary of State in each state.

The report, "Democracy Lost: A Report on the Fatally Flawed 2016 Democratic Primaries," questions the legitimacy of the nomination of Hillary Clinton. It is co-authored by Fritz Scheuren, a professor at George Washington University and the 100th president of the American Statistical Association.

The research has been invited for publication in the Journal of the International Association of Official Statistics (IAOS). The data illustrates the unusually large discrepancies between small and large precinct election returns, and noticeable differences between hand-counted and machine-counted precinct results.

The report: states: *"We conclude by calling for decertification of the 2016 Democratic primary results in every state in which we have established a reasonable doubt as to the accuracy of the vote tally."*

The report cites six major areas of election irregularities in the primary elections:1)Targeting voter suppression, 2) Registration tampering, 3) Illegal voter purges, 4) Exit poll discrepancies, 5) voting machine tampering, 6) Lack of voting machines security.

The report documented how Hillary Clinton's campaign benefited from these *"various types of fraud."* Election Justice USA estimated that 184 pledged delegates were lost by Senator Bernie Sanders as a result of fraud.

There is strong and compelling evidence of election fraud in Alabama, California, Georgia, Illinois, Indiana, Kentucky, Louisiana, Maryland, Mississippi, Missouri, Massachusetts, New Jersey, New Mexico, New York, Ohio, South Carolina and Tennessee

As a remedy for future elections, the report calls for the *"exclusive use of hand-counted paper ballots in all future US elections."* The report mentions the HBO documentary "Hacking Democracy" which shows how a vote-counting machine can be "hacked". A malicious program is inserted in the machine, with or without the knowledge of local election officials, which miscounts the votes on the ballots inserted into the machine. Most voting jurisdictions in the US now use such "optical scan" vote tabulating machines.

Pre-election Polls

Is the **corporate** media reporting Jill Stein's true polling numbers? It appears obvious that the corporate media does not want her in the debates. It would radically change the dynamic of the race.

According to the polls, 12% of respondents are Independents. But the Gallup Party Affiliation Survey indicates the electorate consists of 42% Independents, 29% Democrats and 29% Republicans.

To believe the Media polls, you must believe that Jill Stein has just 5% of Independents and Democrats. In the primaries, Sanders won approximately 65% of Independents and 35% of Democrats. One would logically expect that Stein would do nearly as well as Sanders against Clinton in a four-way race. They are in essential agreement on major issues - and Clinton has very low approval ratings. But Stein had an implausibly low 3% on Aug. 24 and 1% on July 17.

The latest polls show Trump tied with Clinton. The Election Model indicates that he may be leading by 6%. Johnson is taking votes from Trump. If Stein's share increased by 10%, Clinton's would decline accordingly - and Trump would be on his way to a landslide.

In the Aug. 24 *Ipsos / Reuters* poll, Clinton had 39%; Trump 36%; Johnson 7% and Stein 3%. The sample of 1,516 voters included 635 Democrats (41.9%), 527 Republicans (34.8%), 174 Independents (11.5%) and 180 (11.8%) who did not indicate a preference.

The poll also indicated a Party ID split of 36% Democrats and 25% Republicans - an apparent contradiction to the polling sample. Assuming 39% were Independents, it is a close match to the Gallup Survey

Stein needs 15% to qualify for the debates. If Jill got in the debates, her visibility would skyrocket, her poll shares would increase and Hillary Clinton's shares would decline. How many Independent and Democratic voters even know Jill Stein?

Current Media Polls

	Pct	Stein	Clinton	Trump	Johnson
Ind	12%	5%	40%	40%	5%
Dem	44%	5%	85%	5%	5%
Rep	44%	0%	5%	85%	10%
Total	**100%**	**2.8%**	**44.4%**	**44.4%**	**8.4%**

Adjusted Media Poll Shares

	Pct	Stein	Clinton	Trump	Johnson
Ind	12%	30%	15%	40%	15%
Dem	44%	15%	70%	5%	10%
Rep	44%	0%	5%	85%	10%
Total	**100%**	**10.2%**	**34.8%**	**44.4%**	**10.6%**

Election Model – Gallup Party-ID

	Pct	Stein	Clinton	Trump	Johnson
Ind	42%	35%	20%	25%	20%
Dem	29%	20%	70%	5%	5%
Rep	29%	2%	2%	80%	16%
Total	**100%**	**21.1%**	**29.3%**	**35.2%**	**14.4%**

2. Historical Overview

Before the advent of the personal computer, mainframes and minicomputers were programmed by professionals in major corporations. Programming was difficult and time consuming. Computers were used by scientists, engineers, investment bankers and other analytical professionals. Second generation IBM 7094 mainframe took up a full floor of office space.

In 1980, personal computers and spreadsheets became available. In 1982, the groundbreaking Lotus 1-2-3 spreadsheet included limited macro programming and graphics functions. Complex FORTRAN programs were converted to spreadsheets by Wall Street investment banking firms. Simple calculations no longer required time-consuming program development.

The Internet became a gateway to massive databases which could be downloaded by the online user. The necessary tools were now available to analyze election trends using pre-election and exit poll data. The data is compiled and weighted by demographics and turnout.

Unadjusted exit polls made available at poll closing have already been adjusted. The media uses the polls to forecast winners and discuss trends. Some media outlets may make it public. Early/absentee voters are sampled by telephone.

The results are added to the Election Day poll by estimating how much of the total vote is early or absentee.

Edison forces the exit poll to match the official results, by adjusting respondent replies in all demographic categories. The unadjusted polls are compared to the official results. The exit poll discrepancy from the recorded vote is compared to the margin of error to calculate an estimated probability of election fraud.

The unadjusted polls are initially posted on media websites at poll closing. But as the poll is adjusted, the websites are updated. In New York, for example, CNN's exit poll showed Bernie Sanders had 48% at 9:00 PM, but just 42% an hour later. Election fraud benefiting Clinton is the best explanation for what we've seen in the Democratic primaries. Nothing else can explain the exit poll discrepancies, altered registrations, and precinct vote irregularities.

Simple probability calculations confirm that it is mathematically impossible for the exit poll discrepancies to be due to random sampling error or from the above explanations of polling bias. The exit polls clearly reflect voter intent.

Some of the exit polling discrepancies are attributable to large numbers of uncounted provisional ballots. In the Democratic primaries, this is a source of election fraud. Most of the provisional ballots were cast due to voters who had their party registration switched or purged. Nearly all of the voters affected were Sanders supporters, indicating targeted voter registration tampering.

Most exit polling discrepancies cannot be explained by uncounted ballots. Therefore, vote rigging is the most likely explanation. Vote rigging can occur with minimal human involvement. It was confirmed by audit observers in Chicago, raising the likelihood that other jurisdictions had incorrect results.

Exit poll discrepancies caused by vote rigging is further confirmed with a state-by-state analysis. States that are most vulnerable to vote rigging have hackable machines and less effective audit procedures resulting in large exit poll discrepancies. In virtually every state with high exit poll discrepancies, Clinton's cumulative vote share increased with precinct size independent of demographics, indicating that precinct results were rigged in urban and suburban counties with large precincts.

Exit poll data for various demographics are expressed in a table (matrix) of numbers. In a spreadsheet, the table consists of data in cells (column, row). Basic arithmetic operations applied to the matrix are sufficient to prove election fraud.

Actual, raw unadjusted exit poll results are changed in all matrix crosstabs (demographics) to conform to the recorded vote. The crosstab "How Did You Vote in the last election?" has proved to be the Smoking Gun in detecting presidential election fraud from 1988-2008.

In the 1968-2012 Presidential elections, the Republicans won the average recorded vote by 48.7-45.8%. The 1968-2012 National True Vote Model (TVM) indicates the Democrats won the True Vote by 49.6-45.0% – a 7.5% margin discrepancy.

In the 1988-2012 elections, the Democrats won the unadjusted state exit poll aggregate by 52-42%, but the official recorded vote by just 48-46%, an 8% margin discrepancy.

The key to understanding how elections are rigged is to study the exit polls and cumulative vote shares. The pattern keeps repeating: **exit polls are adjusted to match the recorded vote**. The pollsters admit it, but claim the adjustments are made to correct the polls, the assumption being that the recorded vote count is pristine and there is no fraud. At least that is what the pollsters and pundits would like us to believe. But historically, the unadjusted exit polls are very close to the True Vote.

The state exit poll margin of error was (MoE) was exceeded in 135 of 274 state presidential elections from 1988-2008. The probability of the occurrence is ZERO. Only 14 (5%) would be expected to exceed the MoE at the 95% confidence level. Of the 135 which exceeded the MoE, 131 red-shifted to the Republican. The probability P of that anomaly is ABSOLUTE ZERO

The official recorded vote has deviated from the True Vote in every election since 1968 – always favoring the Republicans. Voting machine "glitches" are not due to machine failures; they are caused by malicious programming.

The proof is based on the 1988-2008 Unadjusted State Exit Polls Statistical Reference. Not one political scientist, pollster, statistician, mathematician or media pundit has ever rebutted the data or the calculation itself. They have chosen not to discuss the topic. And who can blame them? Job security is everything.

Election forecasters, academics, political scientists and main stream media pundits never discuss or analyze the statistical evidence that proves election fraud is systemic – beyond a reasonable doubt. Those who never discuss or analyze Election Fraud should focus on the factual statistical data and run the models. If anyone wants to refute the analytic evidence, they are encouraged to do so in a response. Election forecasters, academics and political scientists are welcome to peer review the content.

The bedrock of the evidence derives from this undisputed fact: National and state actual exit poll results are always adjusted in order to force a match to the recorded vote – even if doing so requires an impossible turnout of prior election voters and implausible vote shares.

All demographic categories are adjusted to conform to the recorded vote. To use these forced final exit polls as the basis for election research is unscientific and irresponsible. The research is based on the bogus premise that the recorded vote is sacrosanct and represents how people actually voted. Nothing can be further from the truth.

It is often stated that exit polls were very accurate in elections prior to 2004 but have deviated sharply from the recorded vote since. That is a misconception. UNADJUSTED exit polls have ALWAYS been accurate; they closely matched the True Vote Model in the 1988-2008 presidential elections. The adjusted, published exit polls have always matched the fraudulent RECORDED vote because they have been forced to. That's why they APPEAR to have been accurate.

The Census Bureau indicates that since 1968 approximately 80 million more votes were cast than recorded. And these were just the uncounted votes. What about the votes switched on unverifiable voting machines and central tabulators? But vote miscounts are only part of the story. The True Vote analysis does not include the millions of potential voters who were illegally disenfranchised and never got to vote.

In 1988, Bush defeated Dukakis by 7 million recorded votes. But approximately 11 million ballots (75% Democratic) were uncounted. Dukakis won the unadjusted exit polls in 24 battleground states by 51-47% and the unadjusted National Exit Poll by 50-49%. The classic book Vote Scam provided evidence that the voting machines were rigged for Bush.

In 1992, Clinton defeated Bush by 5.8 million recorded votes (43.0-37.5%). Approximately 9 million were uncounted. The National Exit Poll was forced to match the recorded vote with an impossible 119% turnout of living 1988 Bush voters in 1992. The unadjusted state exit polls had Clinton winning a 16 million vote landslide (47.6-31.7%). The True Vote Model indicates that he won by 51-30% with 19% voting for third party candidate Ross Perot.

In 1996, Clinton defeated Dole by 8.6 million recorded votes (49.3-40.7%); 9 million were uncounted. The unadjusted state exit polls (70,000 respondents) had Clinton winning a 16 million vote landslide (52.6-37.1%). The True Vote Model indicates that he had 53.6%.

In 2000, Al Gore won by 540,000 recorded votes (48.4-47.9%). But the unadjusted state exit polls (58,000 respondents) indicated that he won by 50.8-44.4%, a 6 million vote margin. There were nearly 6 million uncounted votes. The True Vote Model had Gore by 51.5-44.7%. The Supreme Court awarded the election to Bush (271-267 EV). In Florida, 185,000 ballots were uncounted. Twelve states flipped from Gore in the exit poll to Bush in the recorded vote: AL AR AZ CO FL GA MO NC NV TN TX VA. Gore would have won the election if he captured just one of the states. Democracy died in 2000.

In July 2004 I began posting weekly Election Model projections based on the state and national polls. The model was the first to use Monte Carlo Simulation and sensitivity analysis to calculate the probability of winning the electoral vote. The final projection had Kerry winning 337 electoral votes with 51.8% of the two-party vote, closely matching the unadjusted exit polls.

The adjusted 2004 National Exit Poll was mathematically impossible; it was forced to match Kerry's 48.3% recorded vote (the unadjusted NEP indicated that Kerry had 51.7%). The adjusted poll indicated that there were 52.6 million returning Bush 2000 voters (43% of the 122.3 million recorded). But Bush had just 50.5 million votes in 2000; only 48 million were alive in 2004. Assuming a 96% turnout, 46 million voted. Therefore, simple arithmetic shows that the adjusted NEP overstated the number of returning Bush voters by 6.6 (52.6-46) million. In order to match the recorded vote, there had to be an impossible 110% turnout of living Bush 2000 voters.

The exit pollsters had to switch 471 (6.7%) of Kerry's 7,064 responders to Bush in order to match the recorded vote. Kerry had 51% at 4pm (8,349 respondents). His exit poll share increased to 51.7% at the final 13,660.

The ultimate proof that the election was stolen is confirmed by Kerry's 4 million new voter margin (22 million new voters, nearly 60% for Kerry), b) 4 million returning Gore voter margin and c) 2 million returning Nader voter margin.

The post-election True Vote Model calculated a feasible turnout of living 2000 voters based on Census total votes cast (recorded plus net uncounted), a 1.25% annual mortality rate and 98% Gore/Bush voter turnout. It determined that Kerry won by 67-57 million and had 379 EV. Kerry's unadjusted state exit poll aggregate 51.0% share was close to his 51.7% unadjusted National Exit Poll share. He had 53.5% in the True Vote Model. There was further confirmation of a Kerry landslide by 10 million votes. Consider the adjustments made to the 2004 National Exit Poll crosstabs to force a match to the recorded vote.

2004 Adjusted National Exit Poll (Recorded Vote)

2000	Turnout	Mix	Kerry	Bush	Other	Alive	Turnout
DNV	20,790	17%	54%	44%	2%	-	-
Gore	45,249	37%	90%	10%	0%	48,454	93%
Bush	52,586	43%	9%	91%	0%	47,933	110%
Other	3,669	3%	64%	14%	22%	3,798	97%
Total	122,294	100%	48.27%	50.73%	1.00%	100,185	94%

			Kerry	Bush	Other
Total Votes			59,031	62,040	1,223

Unadjusted NEP

2000	Voted	Mix	Kerry	Bush	Other
DNV	23,116	18.4%	57%	41%	2%
Gore	48,248	38.4%	91%	8%	1%
Bush	49,670	39.5%	10%	90%	0%
Other	4,703	3.7%	64%	17%	19%
Total	125,737	100%	51.8%	46.8%	1.5%
Total Votes			65,070	58,829	1,838

True Vote

(Plausible 2000 returning voter mix)					
2000	Voted	Mix	Kerry	Bush	Other
DNV	22,381	17.8%	57%	41%	2%
Gore	52,055	41.4%	91%	8%	1%
Bush	47,403	37.7%	10%	90%	0%
Other	3,898	3.1%	64%	17%	19%
Total	125,737	100%	53.6%	45.1%	1.4%
Total Votes			67,362	56,666	1,709

Bush had a 48% national approval rating in the final 11 pre-election polls. The Final adjusted National Exit Poll indicated that he had a 53% approval rating. But he had just a 50% rating in the unadjusted state exit poll weighted aggregate. Given the 3% differential, we can assume that the 48% pre-election approval rating was also inflated by 3% and was really 45% – a virtual match to the True Vote Model.

The exit pollsters had to inflate Bush's 48% pre-election average rating by 5% in the NEP in order to match the recorded vote. There was a 0.99 correlation ratio between Bush's state approval and his unadjusted exit poll share.

Similarly, the unadjusted state exit poll Democratic/Republican Party ID split was 38.8-35.1%. In order to force the National Exit Poll to match the recorded vote, it required a bogus 37-37% split. The correlation between state Republican Party ID and the Bush unadjusted shares was a near-perfect 0.93. This chart displays the state unadjusted Bush exit poll share, approval ratings and Party-ID.

The Final 2006 National Exit Poll indicated that the Democrats had a 52-46% vote share. The Generic Poll Trend Forecasting Model projected that the Democrats would capture 56.43% of the vote. It was within 0.06% of the unadjusted exit poll.

In 2008, Obama had 61% in the unadjusted National Exit Poll (17,836 respondents), but just a 52.9% recorded share. The pollsters had to reduce Obama's respondents from 10873 to 9430 (13.3%) in order to force a match to his 52.9% recorded vote.

The 2008 Election Model projection exactly matched Obama's 365 electoral votes and was within 0.2% of his 52.9% share (a 9.5 million margin). But the model understated his True Vote. The forecast was based on final likely voter (LV) polls that had Obama leading by 7%. The registered voter (RV) polls had him up by 13% – before undecided voter allocation. The landslide was denied.

The Final 2008 National Exit Poll was forced to match the recorded vote by indicating an impossible 103% turnout of living Bush 2004 voters and 12 million more returning Bush than Kerry voters. Given Kerry's 5% unadjusted 2004 exit poll and 8% True Vote margin, one would expect 7 million more returning Kerry than Bush voters – a 19 million discrepancy from the Final 2008 NEP. Another anomaly:

The Final 2008 NEP indicated there were 5 million returning third party voters – but only 1.2 million were recorded in 2004. Either the

2008 NEP or the 2004 recorded third-party vote share (or both) was wrong. The True Vote Model determined that Obama won by over 22 million votes with 420 EV. His 58% share was within 0.1% of the unadjusted state exit poll aggregate (83,000 respondents).

2008 Adjusted National Exit Poll (Recorded Vote)

	2004 Implied	2008 Votes	Mix	Obama	McCain	Other
DNV	-	17.1	13%	71%	27%	2%
Kerry	42.5%	48.6	37%	89%	9%	2%
Bush	52.9%	60.5	46%	17%	82%	1%
Other	4.6%	5.3	4%	72%	26%	2%
	Total	131.5	100%	52.9%	45.6%	1.5%
	Votes	131.5		69.5	59.9	2.1

2008 Unadjusted Exit Poll

Voted 2004	2004 Implied	2008 Votes	Mix	Obama	McCain	Other
		Exact match to TVM & unadj state				
DNV	-	17.7	13.4%	71%	27%	2%
Kerry	50.2%	57.1	43.4%	89%	9%	2%
Bush	44.6%	50.8	38.6%	17%	82%	1%
Other	5.2%	5.9	4.5%	72%	26%	2%
	Total	131.5	100%	58.0%	40.3%	1.7%
	Votes	131.5		76.3	53.0	2.2

2008 True Vote model

	2004 Implied	2008 Votes	Mix	Obama	McCain	Other
DNV	-	15.3	11.7%	71%	27%	2%
Kerry	53.7%	62.4	47.5%	89%	9%	2%
Bush	45.3%	52.6	40.0%	17%	82%	1%
Other	1.0%	1.2	0.88%	72%	26%	2%
	Total	131.5	100%	58.0%	40.4%	1.6%
	Votes Votes	131.5		76.2	53.2	2.1

In 2012, Obama won the recorded vote by 51.0-47.2% (5.0 million vote margin) and once again overcame the built-in 5% fraud factor. The 2012 Presidential True Vote and Election Fraud Simulation Model exactly forecast Obama's 332 electoral vote based on the state pre-election polls. The True Vote Model projected that Obama would win by 56-42% with 391 electoral votes. But just 31 states were exit polled. A comparison between the True Vote Model and the state and national unadjusted exit polls (i.e. the red-shift) is not possible.

Obama won the 11.7 million votes recorded after Election Day by 58-38%. In 2008, he won the 10.2 million late votes by 59-37%. The slight 2% margin difference is a powerful indicator that if a full set of 2012 unadjusted state and national exit polls were available, they would most likely show that Obama had a 56% True Vote share.

2012 True Vote (millions)

2008	Nat Exit Poll	%	Alive	2012 Turn	Cast	Vote Mix	2-party projection assumes returning voters based on 2008 exit poll			
							BO	MR	BO	MR
Obama	76.2	58.0	72.4	95%	68.8	54.2%	90%	10%	61,9	6,9
McCain	53.0	40.3	50.4	95%	47.8	37.7%	7%	93%	3.3	44.5
Other	2.2	1.7	2.08	95%	1.97	1.5%	50%	50%	1.0	1.0
DNV	-	-	-	-	8.24	6.5%	59%	41%	4.9	3.4
						True	56.0%	44.0%	70.7	55.8
						Recd	51.1%	47.1%	64.8	59.7

2012 Recorded Vote

2008	Recd	%	Alive	2012 Turn	Cast	2-party projection assumes returning voters based on 2008 recorded vote			
						Mix	BO	MR	BO	MR
Obama	69.5	52.9	65.98	95%	62.7	49.4%	90%	10%	56.4	6.3
McCain	59.0	45.6	56.94	95%	54.1	42.6%	7%	93%	3.8	50.3
Other	2.0	1.5	1.87	95%	1.8	1.4%	50%	50%	0.9	0.9
DNV	-	-	-	-	8.24	6.5%	53.7%	46.3%	4.4	3.8
						Proj	51.7%	48.4%	65.5	61.3
						Recd	51.1%	47.0%	64.9	59.7

The 2008 Primary

The exit poll discrepancies in the 2016 Democratic primary were similar to 2008.

Hillary thought she would have the nomination locked up by Super Tuesday, Feb.5. The GOP wanted to run against her. But Obama proved to be a much tougher opponent than either the GOP or Clinton ever expected. Beginning with her miraculous New Hampshire "win", there was an effort to pad her votes. The media did not discuss the many indications of election fraud.

Obama led the exit polls in 21 primaries by 50.4-45.8%. Clinton led 48.4-47.1% in the recorded vote- a 5.9% discrepancy. The exit poll vote shift favored Clinton in 18 of the 21 primaries and the margin of error was exceeded in 11 states. The probability that the discrepancies were due to chance is effectively zero.

Like Sanders, Obama did much better in the caucuses than in machine-counted primaries. Obama's won the primaries (49-47%) and the caucuses (66-34%). But his recorded vote margin was dwarfed by his lead in the exit polls. The progressive candidate always does better in the exit polls than in the vote count. The exit poll discrepancies would be expected to be equally distributed between the two parties. The fact that they virtually always move in favor of the most conservative candidate indicates likely fraud.

Obama led Clinton by over 700,000 in the recorded vote and by over 160 in pledged delegates. But if the exit polls and caucuses reflect the True Vote, he would be leading by more than 1.5 million votes. That would make a tremendous difference in his pledged delegate margin.

Just before the March 4 Texas and Ohio primaries, Rush Limbaugh called for "Operation Chaos" to get Republicans to cross over and vote for Clinton. There have been two groups of Republican crossover voters. The first consists of Republican moderates who voted 2-1 for Obama. The second were Republicans who voted for Clinton due to Operation Chaos.

After March 4, Republican crossover voters increased from 6% to 9%. The change was to Clinton's benefit. Assuming the first 6% of Republicans voted 59-28% for Obama, the other 3% (150,000) were Operation Chaos crossovers who voted 100% for Clinton!

Operation Chaos was one factor that may have caused Obama to lose the Texas primary by 51-47%. It definitely caused his 50.6-49.4% defeat in Indiana. Of course, the effect on pledged delegates was minimal.

New Hampshire: The Final pre-election polls (3-4% MoE) gave Obama an average 8% margin over HRC. The early (unadjusted) exit poll had Obama winning by 8%. He won New Hampshire hand-counts by 5.90% but lost machine-counts by exactly the same margin. Given that Obama led the poll at 8pm by 39-36%, what was the probability that HRC would win the official vote by at least 3% (39-36%)? Assume that the exit poll margin of error was 1.5%. The probability P of vote miscount is P=.0044% = normdist (.39, .36, .015/1.96, true)

Super Tuesday: Just like the 2004 battleground states exit poll red-shift to Bush, Clinton's recorded vote share in 14 of 16 primaries exceeded her exit poll share. In New York, over 80 precincts, many in black areas, recorded Zero votes for Obama. In Los Angeles, 90,000 independent votes were uncounted due to the confusing ballot design (shades of the infamous Florida 2000 "Butterfly" which cost Gore over 3,000 votes).

Ohio: Clinton's vote share exceeded her 9pm exit poll share by 3.6% (55.2-51.6%). She won the recorded vote by 10.6% (55.3-44.7%) over Obama. But her exit poll margin was just 3.4% (51.7-48.3%). As always, the Final Exit Poll was adjusted to match the vote count. In addition, there is concrete evidence that Republican cross-over voters played a significant role in delivering votes to Clinton. In

Cuyahoga County 17,000 Republicans followed Rush Limbaugh's advice and voted for her and did in many other counties.

Texas: Zero votes were cast for Republicans in 21 counties (36,239 ballots for Democrats). Zero votes were cast for Democrats in 3 counties (1865 ballots for Republicans). Did Republicans follow Rush Limbaugh's advice and cross over to vote for Clinton?

Mississippi: Obama won by 61-37%, but 25% of Clinton's votes were from Republicans (Operation Chaos). Obama won 65% of Democrats and Independents.

Pennsylvania: Dirty tricks caused votes (and pledged delegates) to be stolen from Obama. Hillary won the recorded vote by 54.7-45.3%. But 100% of the votes were machine-counted. The unadjusted, "pristine" early exit poll had Obama leading 52-47%. His 5% exit poll margin became a 9% recorded vote loss. Clinton led the adjusted exit poll by 52-47. The Final exit poll matched the recorded vote 54-45.

Indiana: The media claimed that Rush Limbaugh's Operation Chaos had no effect on the Indiana primary. Their argument is that the Clinton-Obama (53-47) share of the 10% Republican crossover vote is virtually the same as the split in the total vote. Clinton won by 50.6-49.4%, but Operation Chaos Republican crossovers inflated her vote by 4%. Obama should have been a 51.5-48.5% winner.

3. Analytical Models

Discrepancies between the official recorded vote and unadjusted exit polls are in one direction only. A total of 232 polls shifted from the poll to the vote in favor of the Republican. Only 42 shifted to the Democrat. There should have been an equal shift. The Margin of Error was exceeded in 135 of 274 state presidential exit polls. Only 14 would normally be expected. Of the 135, 131 moved in favor of the Republicans, 4 to the Democrat.

The Binomial distribution is used to calculate that probability that 232 of 274 would red-shift to the GOP: 9.1E-35 (less than 1 in a trillion trillion).

The True Vote Model (TVM) is based on Census votes cast, mortality, prior election voter turnout and National Exit Poll vote shares. The TVM closely matched the exit polls in each election. In 2008, it was within 0.1% of Obama's 58.0% unadjusted exit poll share.The TVM is confirmed by the unadjusted exit polls. There was a massive 8% discrepancy between the exit polls (52D-42R) and the recorded vote (48D-46R). The Probability is calculated by the Normal distribution.

P = 8E-10 = 1- Normdist (0.52, 0.48, 0.012/1.96, true)
P = 1 in 1.2 billion

The Poisson distribution function calculates the probability in which each event has a very low probability of occurrence. The probability P that 131 of 274 would red-shift beyond the margin of error is **P = E-116 P = Poisson (131, .025*274, false).**

P = .0000000000 0000000000 0000000000 0000000000 0000000000 0000000000 0000000000 0000000000 0000000000 0000000000 0000000000 000001

Election Fraud Probabilities – Democratic Primary

The probability P that Sanders would do better in the exit poll than the recorded vote in at least n=24 of N= 26 primaries is given by the **Binomial distribution:**

P = 1 -BINOMDIST (n-1, N, 0.5, true).
P = 1 in 190,000 = 1-BINOMDIST (23, 26, 0.5, true).

The **margin of error** (MoE) is a function of the 2-party exit poll share (EP), and the number N of respondents. **MoE =1.3*1.96*sqrt (EP*(1-EP)/N)**

The probability P that at least n=11 of N=26 primaries would exceed the MoE for a Sanders is calculated using the Binomial distribution:

P = 1- BINOMDIST (n-1, N, 0.025, true)
P = 1 in 76.8 Billion = 1-BINOMDIST (10, 26, 0.025, true)

The probability of fraud in a given primary is calculated using the **Normal distribution.**

P = NORMDIST (EP, RS, MoE /1.96, true) where EP is the exit poll share and RS is the recorded vote share.

For example, the probability of the Ohio exit poll discrepancy:
N=1670 respondents, MoE = 3.12%.
Sanders 2-party EP= 48.1%, RS =43.1%

P= 99.9% = NORMDIST (.481, .431, .0312/1.96, true)

The probability is based on the difference (DIFF) between the exit poll share (EP) and the recorded share (RS) less the MoE: DIFF = EP- RS – MoE. If DIFF = MoE, the probability is 97.5%. The average probability of fraud in the 26 primaries is 97.4%.

Sanders Exit Poll Discrepancy Probabilities

Primary	MoE	Vote	Share	Exit Poll	Diff	Prob
AL	3.93%	386,327	19.8%	25.9%	6.1%	99.9%
AR	4.00%	209,448	31.0%	33.3%	2.3%	87.3%
AZ	3.89%	399,097	40.9%	63.0%	22.1%	100.0%
CT	3.64%	322,658	45.6%	47.2%	1.7%	81.3%
FL	3.03%	1,664,003	34.1%	36.0%	2.0%	90.2%
GA	3.37%	757,340	28.3%	33.8%	5.5%	99.9%
IL	3.48%	1,978,937	49.1%	51.2%	2.0%	87.5%
IN	3.48%	636,024	52.8%	55.4%	2.6%	92.9%
MA	3.53%	1,190,500	49.3%	53.3%	4.0%	98.7%
MD	4.13%	815,356	33.3%	33.4%	0.1%	52.7%
MI	3.27%	1,161,334	50.8%	53.2%	2.4%	92.2%
MO	4.42%	619,673	49.9%	51.9%	2.0%	81.0%
MS	3.36%	218,566	16.6%	21.3%	4.7%	99.7%
NC	3.03%	1,076,699	42.8%	43.7%	0.9%	72.3%
NH	2.64%	246,836	61.4%	60.4%	-1.0%	22.7%
NY	3.52%	1,790,083	42.1%	48.0%	5.9%	100.0%
OH	3.12%	1,192,815	43.1%	48.1%	5.0%	99.9%
OK	4.47%	313,392	55.5%	50.9%	-4.6%	2.1%
PA	3.50%	1,638,560	43.6%	45.1%	1.5%	80.6%
SC	3.09%	367,491	26.1%	31.3%	5.2%	100.0%
TN	3.96%	365,637	32.9%	35.5%	2.6%	90.0%

TX	3.45%	1,410,641	33.7%	37.9%	4.2%	99.1%
VA	3.33%	778,865	35.4%	37.4%	2.0%	88.4%
VT	2.28%	134,198	86.3%	86.5%	0.2%	55.5%
WI	2.99%	992,865	56.7%	63.6%	6.9%	100.0%
WV	4.65%	204,407	51.4%	57.4%	6.0%	99.4%

2004 vs. 2016

In 2004, Bush won the recorded vote by 50.7-48.3%, a 3 million vote margin. Kerry won the National Exit Poll by 51.7-47.0%, a 6 million margin.

The following states flipped from Kerry in the exit poll to Bush in the recorded vote: CO FL IA MO NM NV OH VA.

2004: the average state exit poll margin of error was 3.43%;

2016: the average primary exit poll MoE was 3.52%;

2004: 22 of 50 (44%) exit polls exceeded the MoE for Kerry.

2016: 11 of 26 exit polls (42%) exceeded the MoE for Sanders.

2004: 42 of 50 exit polls (84%) shifted to Bush in the vote.

Note: If AZ, WI, CT preliminary exit polls are included, then 13 of 26 exit polls exceeded the MoE. The probability is 1.2E-14 or less than 1 in 80 trillion!

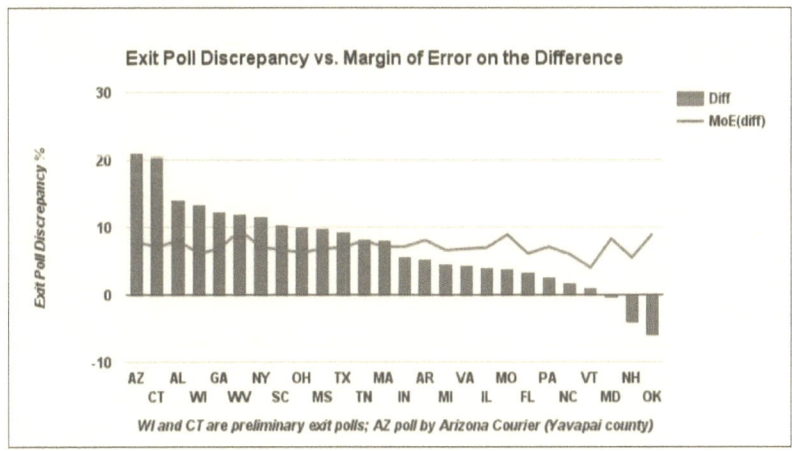

Cumulative Vote Shares

The analysis of cumulative vote shares (CVS) has revealed a consistent pattern. Democrats are the majority in highly populated urban locations; the largest precincts are usually Democratic. Republicans are heavily represented in rural areas. But in scores of state elections there has been an increase in cumulative Republican vote shares in larger precincts. This anomaly has been noted by PhDs in Kansas and Vanderbilt University.

Many counties saw Clinton's vote share significantly increase with precinct size. Demographics fail to explain the trend, indicating that a vote rigging algorithm is inflating Clinton's share in larger precincts. And almost all of the states with substantial exit poll discrepancies show this irregular pattern. Clinton represents the establishment and could be viewed as the Republican in the primary while Sanders, the progressive, can be viewed as the Democrat

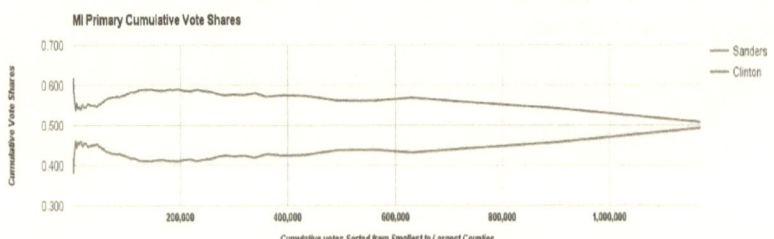

Wichita State University engineering professor and statistician Beth Clarkson has accused three states — Wisconsin, Ohio, & Kansas — of voting irregularities that indicate a tampering of electronic voting machines.

A Vanderbilt Univ. statistical study of precinct level data in US presidential elections reveals a correlation of large precincts and increased fraction of Republican votes.

Fractionalized votes and GEMS election management

http://blackboxvoting.org/fraction-magic-1/

Bev Harris is a writer and founder of Black Box Voting. She has researched and written about election transparency and computerized voting systems since 2002. Harris was featured in the Emmy-nominated HBO documentary Hacking Democracy, and is the author of Black Box Voting: Ballot Tampering in the 21st Century. Harris's research has been covered in The New York Times, Vanity Fair, Time Magazine, CNN and several international publications.

Bennie Smith is a Memphis-based application developer for an electrical manufacturing company. He is also a political strategist who has developed a micro-targeting application that predicts voter turnout. Smith researched how votes that originate from the same source can change once they get into the GEMS vote tabulation program. Smith uncovered a vote tampering mechanism and provided a new approach for analyzing questionable election results.

The GEMS election management system counts approximately 25 percent of all votes in the United States. The results of this study demonstrate that a fractional vote feature is embedded in each GEMS application which can be used to invisibly, yet radically, alter election outcomes by pre-setting desired vote percentages to redistribute votes. This tampering is not visible to election observers, even if they are standing in the room and watching the computer. Use of the decimalized vote feature is unlikely to be detected by auditing or canvass procedures, and can be applied across large jurisdictions in less than 60 seconds.

GEMS vote-counting systems are and have been operated under five trade names: Global Election Systems, Diebold Election Systems, Premier Election Systems, Dominion Voting Systems, and Election Systems & Software, in addition to a number of private regional subcontractors.

Fractionalized vote: the vote is allowed to be 1/2, or 1+7/8, or any other value that is not a whole number. Weighting a race removes the principle of "one person-one vote" to allow some votes to be counted as less than one or more than one. Regardless of what the real votes are, candidates can receive a set percentage of votes. Results can be controlled. For example, Candidate A can be assigned 44% of the votes, Candidate B 51%, and Candidate C the rest.

GEMS fractionalizes votes in three places:
1. *The "Summary" vote tally, which provides overall election totals for each race on Election Night*
2. *The "Statement of Votes Cast", which provides detailed results by precinct and voting method (ie. Polling, absentee, early, provisional)*
3. *The "undervote" count*

Fractions in results reports are not visible. Votes containing decimals are reported as whole numbers unless specifically instructed to reveal decimals (which is not the default setting). All evidence that fractional values ever existed can be removed instantly even from the underlying database using a setting in the GEMS data tables, in which case even instructing GEMS to show the decimals will fail to reveal they were used.

Source code: Instructions to treat votes as decimal values instead of whole numbers are inserted multiple times in the GEMS source code itself; thus, this feature cannot have been created by accident.

Fractionalizing the votes which create the Summary Results allows alteration of Election Night results and results sent to the Secretary of State, as well as results available at and local election officials.

Paper Ballots

Axel Geijsel of Tilburg University (the Netherlands) and Rodolfo Cortes Barragan of Stanford University reported that their analysis found that primary election results in states without a paper trail overwhelmingly favored Hillary Clinton 65-35%. Sanders led Clinton 51-49% in states with a paper trail.

Hand counted ballots show a consistently higher percentage for Sanders. There are two possible explanations for this: the machines are counting the votes differently and the voters forced to use provisional ballots were targeted Sanders voters. The data indicates the footprint of manipulation in the election, and calls into question the validity of the reported results.

The following calculations in the Democratic Primaries spreadsheet shows that Sanders had 47.8% in states with a paper trail and 33.3% in states without a trail. He had 52.6% in exit polls of paper trail states and 37.5% in states without a paper trail.

10 States -No Paper trail		Clinton	Sanders	Margin
Reported	Average	65.4%	33.3%	32.1%
2-party	Reported	66.2%	33.8%	32.5%
2-party	Unadjusted	62.5%	37.5%	25.1%
2-party	Discrepancy	3.7%	-3.7%	7.4%
14 States - Paper trail				
Reported	Average	50.4%	47.8%	2.6%
2-party	Reported	51.3%	48.7%	2.7%
2-party	Unadjusted	47.4%	52.6%	-5.2%
2-party	Discrepancy	3.9%	-3.9%	7.9%
Paper vs. No paper				**15.3%**

Adjusted Exit Poll discrepancies

Democratic primary exit polls were adjusted to match the recorded vote to within 0.06%. The average margin of error was 3.5% for the 26 unadjusted polls. This confirms what we already know: Unadjusted exit polls are always forced to match the recorded vote. The premise is that there is ZERO fraud. View the adjusted polls: http://www.cnn.com/election/primaries/polls

The Gender crosstab is the basis for calculating adjusted vote shares. Exit poll naysayers proclaim that the exit polls are not designed to forecast a winner. But the pollsters ask males and females who they just voted for. Isn't that the same thing as forecasting the winner?

View the calculations to determine the discrepancies in this spreadsheet:
https://docs.google.com/spreadsheets/d/1sGxtIofohrj3POpwq-85Id2_fYKgvgoWbPZacZw0XIY/edit#gid=1591963017

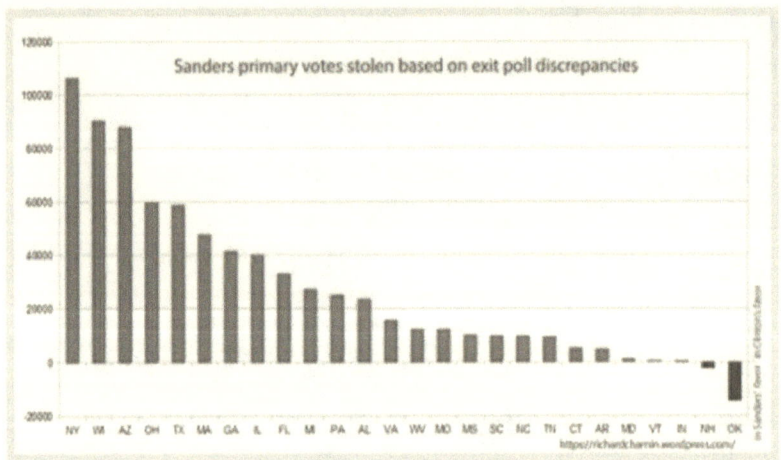

TDMS|RESEARCH

www.tdmsresearch.com

EXIT POLLS VERSUS REPORTED VOTE COUNT. DEMOCRATIC PARTY 2016 PRIMARIES

Democratic Party Clinton v. Sanders	CNN PUBLISHED EXIT POLLS (EP) [1]					REPORTED VOTE COUNT (VC) [2]			EP / VC DISCREPANCIES	
	CLINTON EP	SANDERS EP	MARGIN CLINTON - SANDERS	NUMBER RESPONDE-NTS	TSE [3] ON THE DIFFERENCE	CLINTON VC	SANDERS VC	MARGIN CLINTON - SANDERS	MARGIN DISCREPANCY IN FAVOR OF CLINTON	DISCREPANCY GREATER THAN EP TSE
ALABAMA	70.6%	25.9%	44.7%	806	8.0%	77.84%	19.19%	58.7%	14.0%	6.0%
GEORGIA	64.8%	33.8%	31.0%	1,277	6.8%	71.33%	28.16%	43.2%	12.2%	5.3%
WEST VIRGINIA [4]	42.6%	57.4%	-14.8%	734	9.5%	48.61%	51.39%	-2.8%	12.0%	2.6%
NEW YORK	52.0%	47.6%	4.3%	1,307	7.1%	57.99%	42.01%	16.0%	11.6%	4.5%
SOUTH CAROLINA [5]	68.4%	31.2%	37.2%	1,328	6.6%	73.48%	25.97%	47.5%	10.3%	3.7%
OHIO	51.4%	47.6%	3.8%	1,670	6.3%	56.50%	42.70%	13.8%	10.0%	3.7%
MISSISSIPPI	77.7%	21.3%	56.3%	966	6.8%	82.63%	16.46%	66.2%	9.9%	3.0%
TEXAS	60.6%	37.9%	22.7%	1,282	7.0%	65.20%	33.20%	32.0%	9.3%	2.3%
TENNESSEE	60.9%	35.5%	25.4%	949	8.0%	66.11%	32.43%	33.7%	8.3%	0.3%
MASSACHUSETTS	45.7%	52.3%	-6.6%	1,297	7.1%	50.11%	48.69%	1.4%	8.0%	0.9%
INDIANA	44.6%	55.4%	-10.7%	1,323	7.1%	47.50%	52.50%	-5.0%	5.7%	
ARKANSAS	64.7%	33.3%	31.4%	900	8.1%	66.29%	29.74%	36.6%	5.2%	
MICHIGAN	45.9%	52.1%	-6.2%	1,510	6.6%	48.27%	49.83%	-1.6%	4.6%	
VIRGINIA	62.2%	37.4%	24.8%	1,370	6.8%	64.29%	35.19%	29.1%	4.3%	
ILLINOIS	48.4%	50.7%	-2.3%	1,341	7.0%	50.46%	48.72%	1.7%	4.1%	
MISSOURI	47.4%	51.1%	-3.7%	831	8.9%	49.60%	49.40%	0.2%	3.9%	
FLORIDA	63.7%	35.9%	27.9%	1,632	6.1%	64.50%	33.30%	31.2%	3.4%	
PENNSYLVANIA	54.5%	45.1%	9.4%	1,313	7.1%	55.58%	43.56%	12.0%	2.6%	
CONNECTICUT	50.4%	47.2%	3.2%	1,223	7.3%	51.80%	46.42%	5.4%	2.2%	
NORTH CAROLINA	53.8%	41.7%	12.1%	1,744	6.0%	54.60%	40.80%	13.8%	1.7%	
VERMONT	12.9%	86.5%	-73.6%	1,453	4.6%	13.62%	86.10%	-72.5%	1.1%	
MARYLAND	63.8%	33.4%	30.4%	848	8.3%	63.03%	33.25%	29.8%	-0.6%	
WISCONSIN	43.5%	55.0%	-11.5%	1,681	6.2%	43.11%	56.57%	-13.5%	-2.0%	
NEW HAMPSHIRE [6]	40.4%	58.6%	-18.2%	2,089	5.5%	37.95%	60.40%	-22.4%	-4.2%	
OKLAHOMA	46.6%	50.9%	-4.3%	811	9.0%	41.52%	51.87%	-10.3%	-6.1%	
Pending Confirmation:										
WISCONSIN [7]	36.5%	63.4%	-26.9%	1,681	6.1%	43.11%	56.57%	-13.5%	13.4%	7.3%
CONNECTICUT [8]	40.0%	55.0%	-15.0%	1,223	7.1%	51.80%	46.42%	5.4%	20.4%	13.3%

February 9 - May 10, 2016 Primaries*   Table and notes by Theodore de Macedo Soares   Contact email: tdms@tdmsresearch.com

Democratic Primary True Vote Model

There were 25 Democratic primary exit polls and 2 entrance polls. Clinton won the average adjusted exit poll (the recorded vote) by 56.6-43.4%.

The True Vote Model (TVM) base case estimate is that Sanders had 52.3% of the total vote in primaries and caucuses and likely won an estimated 37 primaries and caucuses. The TVM assumes that the Gallup survey of voter preference reflects actual turnout. This was not the case in closed primaries.

Over a million prospective Sanders voters never voted. The model assumes Sanders had 75% of the estimated 20% of voters who were disenfranchised (voter registrations switched or dropped, provisional ballots, etc.).

The TVM uses a combination of adjusted exit poll vote shares and Gallup Party ID survey percentages. So Bernie must have done better than his average 52.3% share. Party-ID for each state is estimated based on the proportional change in national Party-ID from 2014 to 2016. The 2-party share of Independents increased from 37.4% to 57.3%.

The base case model assumptions:
1. Sanders won the caucuses with 63.9% (based on 2014 turnout).
2. Clinton had 51.7% in 26 exit polled primaries
3. Sanders won 75% of uncounted provisional ballots
4. 10% of Sanders' votes flipped to Clinton in primaries not exit polled.

The model indicates that Bernie won 17 of 27 exit polled primaries (including the NV and IA entrance poll caucuses), 8 of 12 primaries where there were no exit polls (CA KY MT NM SD DE RI OR) and all 12 caucuses with a 65% average share.

Impossible or implausible Sanders and Clinton shares of Democrats were required to match the recorded vote in a number of primaries. The recorded vote was also impossible or implausible.

Use estimated 2016 Party-ID weights and adjusted exit poll vote shares to calculate Sanders' share of Democrats required to match the recorded vote in 25 adjusted primary exit polls and 2 entrance polls: Given:

- 1- Independent and Democratic Gallup Survey Party-ID
- 2- Recorded vote shares
- 3- Sanders' exit poll share of Independents

Sanders required share of Democrats is...

Impossible in 7 primaries: AL CT SC MS AR FL IA

Implausible in 11: TN GA TX NV VA NY MA NC MD OH PA

Plausible in 9: IN NH MI IL WV MO OK WI VT

This is an indication of election fraud in at least 18 primaries.

NY	Party-ID	Clinton	Sanders
IND	53.0%	28.0%	72.0%
DEM	47.0%	91.8%	8.2%
Total	100.0%	57.9%	42.1%

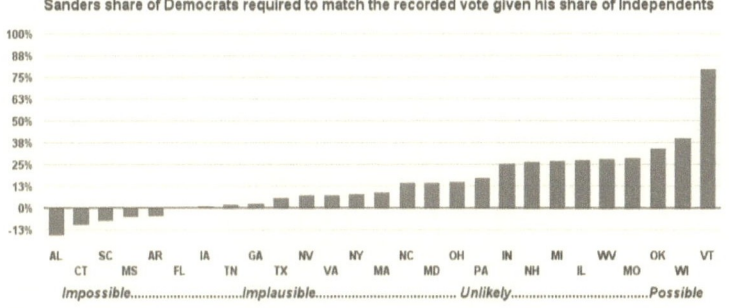

Sanders share of Democrats required to match the recorded vote given his share of Independents

Primary True Vote

This analysis seeks to determine an approximate True Vote in the 2016 Democratic primaries. Clinton led the average of the adjusted exit polls (which were forced to match the recorded vote) by 56.4-43.6%. But there has been a significant increase in Independents National Party-ID statistics since 2014.

The calculation of the True Vote differs from the Recorded Vote (adjusted Exit poll) in just one aspect: Independent and Democratic weights are based on the actual 2016 Party-ID mix. Sanders vote shares are unchanged. In other words the True Vote assumes that no voters were disenfranchised and/or removed from the rolls. In the exit polled primaries, Sanders had a 51.3% True Vote and a 43.6% Recorded Vote.

2014 National Party-ID: Dem 40.5 - Rep 35.2 - Ind 24.2%
2-party mix: Dem 62.6 - Ind 37.4%

Compare to the Gallup Party affiliation monthly survey:
Note the 19% increase in Independents since 2014.

2016 National Party-ID: Dem 32 -Rep 25 -Ind 43%
2-party mix: Independent 57.3- Democrat 42.7%.
http://www.gallup.com/poll/15370/party-affiliation.aspx

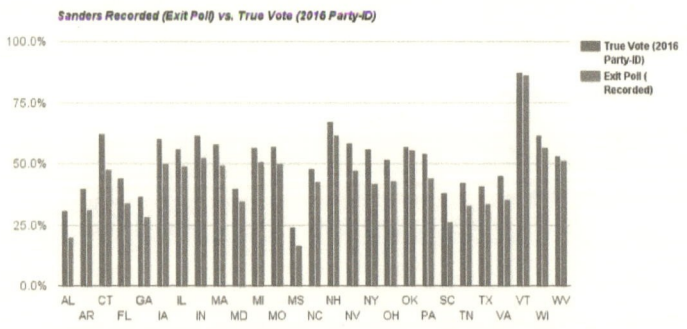

Approval Ratings

In polls from Gallup and Pew, Sanders scored a higher favorability rating than Clinton. The favorability ratings for Sanders consistently outperformed Hillary Clinton, with mixed results in the subgroup of African American voters. In non-paper trail states

Clinton won the African American vote with 83%. In paper-trail states, she had 74% - much closer to the polling results. Sanders outperforms Clinton in almost all groups and subgroups in these polls, in contrast to the recorded votes in the primaries.

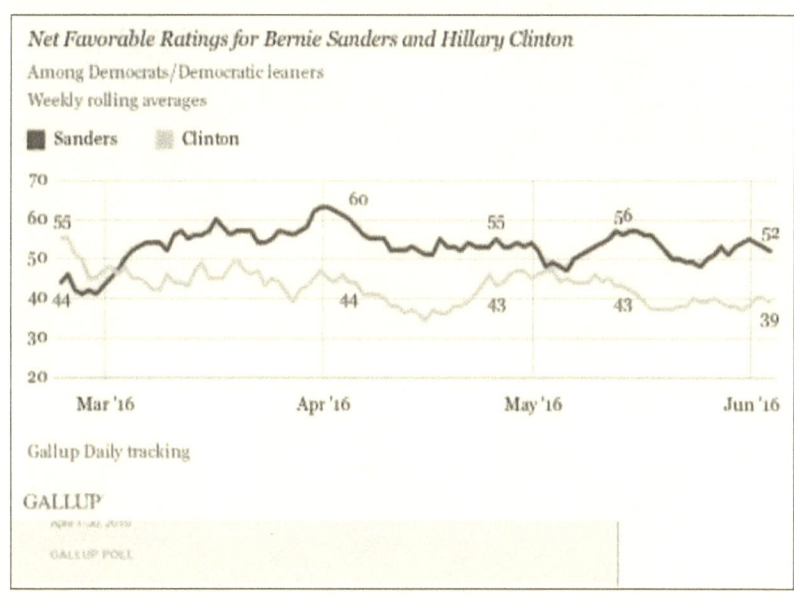

Net Favorable Ratings for Bernie Sanders and Hillary Clinton
Among Democrats/Democratic leaners
Weekly rolling averages

The unadjusted 2004 state exit polls tracked closely to Bush approval ratings. There was a near-perfect 0.99 correlation between them. His approval was highly correlated (0.87) to the monthly pre-election polls.

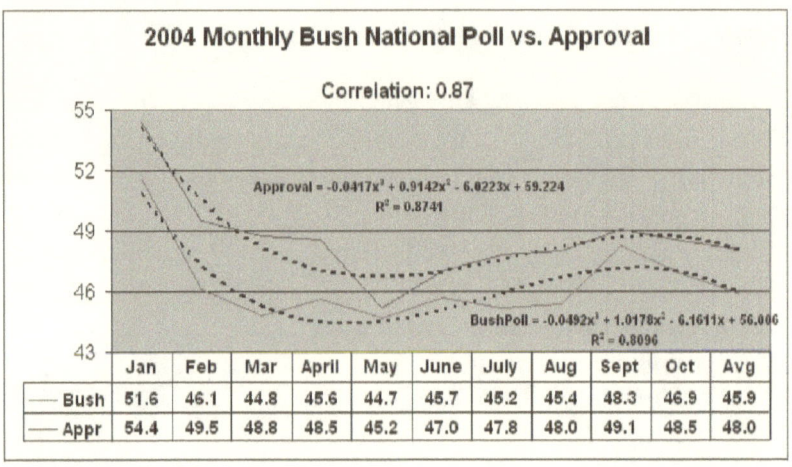

2004 Monthly Bush National Poll vs. Approval

Correlation: 0.87

Approval = $-0.0417x^3 + 0.9142x^2 - 6.0223x + 59.224$
$R^2 = 0.8741$

BushPoll = $-0.0492x^3 + 1.0178x^2 - 6.1611x + 56.006$
$R^2 = 0.8096$

	Jan	Feb	Mar	April	May	June	July	Aug	Sept	Oct	Avg
Bush	51.6	46.1	44.8	45.6	44.7	45.7	45.2	45.4	48.3	46.9	45.9
Appr	54.4	49.5	48.8	48.5	45.2	47.0	47.8	48.0	49.1	48.5	48.0

4. The 2016 Primaries

Iowa and Nevada Caucuses

Iowa and Nevada had entrance polls which were adjusted to match the recorded vote. Clinton won NV by 52.7-47.3% and IA by 50.1-49.9%. The 2-Party-ID split of Democrats and Independents was heavily weighted to the Democrats. The IA and NV caucuses were both close, unlike the other 12 caucuses in which Sanders won landslides.

This analysis indicates that the IA and NV are consistent with the other 12. Applying the Gallup survey split, Sanders won NV with 61.7% and IA with 63.6%.http://www.gallup.com/poll/15370/party-affiliation.aspx

NEVADA
http://www.cnn.com/election/primaries/polls/NV/Dem

	Entrance Poll			Gallup Survey		
Primary	Party-ID	Clinton	Sanders	Party-ID	Clinton	Sanders
IND	19.0%	24.5%	75.5%	60.3%	24.5%	75.5%
DEM	81.0%	59.3%	40.7%	39.7%	59.3%	40.7%
Total	100.0%	52.7%	47.3%	100.0%	38.3%	61.7%

IOWA
http://www.cnn.com/election/primaries/polls/IA/Dem

	Entrance Poll			Gallup Survey		
Primary	Party-ID	Clinton	Sanders	Party-ID	Clinton	Sanders
DEM	76.0%	57.3%	42.7%	30.2%	57.3%	42.7%
Total	100.0%	50.1%	49.9%	100.0%	36.4%	63.6%

Iowa

The Des Moines Register, the largest newspaper in Iowa, called for an audit into the results of the state's Democratic caucus, pointing to confusion and problems at numerous polling sites -- and declaring "something smells in the Democratic Party."

In an editorial, it wrote that "once again the world is laughing at Iowa" over alleged discrepancies and disorganization surrounding caucus results and called the process a "debacle." It pointed to Hillary Clinton's razor-thin margin of victory over Sen. Bernie Sanders in seeking an audit.

"Too many accounts have arisen of inconsistent counts, untrained and overwhelmed volunteers, confused voters, cramped precinct locations, a lack of voter registration forms and other problems. Too many of us, including members of the Register editorial board who were observing caucuses, saw opportunities for error amid Monday night's chaos," the editorial board said. *"The Iowa Democratic Party must act quickly to assure the accuracy of the caucus results, beyond a shadow of a doubt,"* the editorial board wrote.

The editorial comes ahead of an MSNBC-hosted debate in New Hampshire Thursday night, where Clinton and Sanders will face off one-on-one. A day earlier, Sanders questioned the results in interviews.

"The Iowa caucus is so complicated -- it's not 100 percent sure that we didn't win it," Sanders said on NBC's "Today" show Wednesday.

Sanders' Iowa communications director Rania Batrice told Fox News the campaign requested a meeting Wednesday with state Democratic Party officials and was "looking forward to working with the party to address major discrepancies in reporting in order to ensure accurate results are tabulated.

Nevada

A former Congressional candidate in Nevada's fourth district, Dan Rolle, tweeted that starting in 2012, the Nevada Democratic Party began changing the state's voter registration system to rig the caucuses for Clinton. Most state Democratic parties—including Nevada—moved to NGPVAN database systems, which Rolle said facilitated the monopolization of voter data in favor of Clinton. http://observer.com/2016/09/former-democratic-congressional-candidate-says-hillary-stole-nevada/

Rolle's team found between five to 10 percent discrepancies and higher in the voter file. Clinton defeated Sanders in the Nevada caucuses 52.6- 47.3%, a margin lower than the voter file.

A video posted on Youtube revealed unregistered Clinton supporters entering a caucus site in Nevada.

Rolle noted that the caucuses could have easily swung one or two delegates at several different sites. Following the caucuses, 64 of Sanders delegates were rejected at the Nevada State Democratic Party Convention by a board chosen by Clinton. Roberta Lange, the state party's chair, denied a recount of delegates and ended the convention at her own discretion, therefore breaking the party's own rules to ensure that Clinton received more delegates from Nevada than Sanders.

Mainstream media coverage portrayed Sanders supporters as violent. Some went so far as to falsely claim Sanders supporters threw chairs in protest—a narrative Wikileaks proved the DNC staff intentionally pushed to discredit the Sanders campaign. The allegations were eventually debunked, yet *The New York Times*, among other publications, failed to publish retractions or make edits to correct the story. What happened at the Nevada State Convention is essentially a microcosm of the entire Democratic primaries.

Massachusetts: Hand-counts vs. Machine Counts

Clinton won the Massachusetts primary by just 1.4%, but she did well in urban areas. Sanders won hand-counted precincts by 57-40% in 68 Towns (32,360 votes, 2.7% of votes cast). Sanders also had 52.1% in the preliminary exit poll which he won by 52.1-45.7%. His win probability was also 97%.The diverging lines confirm the unadjusted exit poll and indicate fraud.

Late changes to the MA Democratic Primary exit poll indicate that the election was likely stolen. As always, the exit poll was adjusted to match the recorded vote. Sanders led the Unadjusted MA Exit Poll (1297 respondents) by 52.3-45.7%. The poll was captured from CNN at 8:01pm

Clinton led the adjusted exit poll (1406 respondents) by 50.3-48.7%, a near-exact match to the 1.4% RECORDED vote margin. But her 50.3% share was IMPOSSIBLE. The proof is self-explanatory: How could Clinton gain 114 respondents and Sanders just 7 of the final 109 exit poll respondents?

Clinton won by 51-49% on electronic voting machines from ES&S, Diebold and Dominion. Sanders won 68 hand-counted precincts by 58-41%. He won 250 of 351 jurisdictions and had at least 58% in 110. There is a 97% probability that Sanders won the election given the 3.55% Margin of Error. The MoE includes a cluster effect (30% of the 2.72% calculated MoE).

Sanders 53.4% two-party share and the MoE are input to the Normal distribution function to calculate his win probability:

P = 97% = Normdist (.534, 0.5, 1.3* MoE/1.96,true)

Recent Massachusetts elections are highly suspect and show similar anomalies. The True Vote and Registered Voter Turnout models and CVS analysis indicate to a near 100% probability that the 2014 MA Governor election was stolen from Coakley (D).

In the special 2010 senate election for Sen. Kennedy's seat, Coakley won the 71 hand-counted precincts with 51.1% of the vote (32,247) to Brown's 47.8% (30,136). Massachusetts has 71 hand count locations, 91 ES&S and 187 Diebold.

In the 2008 MA primary, Clinton snatched victory from the jaws of defeat, overcoming an Obama 8 point lead in the final pre-election polls. Obama won the hand-counted precincts by the same 5% that Clinton won the machine counts: 52-47%.

Clinton's cumulative vote share increases going from small to large towns. The vote shares should be nearly constant. At the 10% CVS mark, Sanders had 57%. He had 54% at the 25% mark.

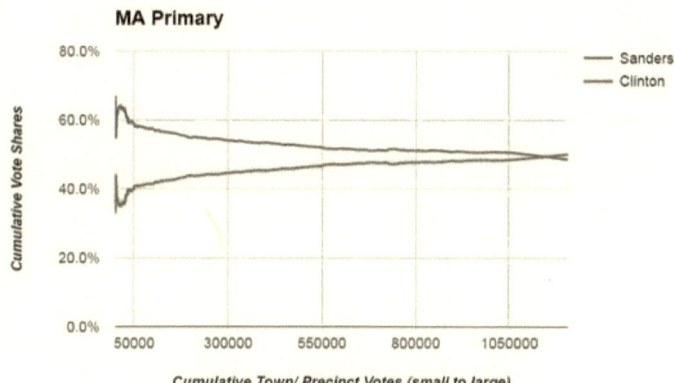

UNADJUSTED MA EXIT POLL

		Sanders	Clinton	Other
Respondents	**1297**	**678**	**593**	**26**
Male	42.0%	61.0%	37.0%	2.0%
Female	58.0%	46.0%	52.0%	2.0%
Total	**100.0%**	**52.3%**	**45.7%**	**2.0%**

ADJUSTED MA EXIT POLL (CNN)

		Sanders	Clinton	Other
Respondents	**1406**	**685**	**707**	**14**
Increase	**109**	**7**	**114**	**-12**
Male	42.0%	58.0%	41.0%	1.0%
Female	58.0%	42.0%	57.0%	1.0%
Total	**100.0%**	**48.7%**	**50.3%**	**1.0%**

Michigan: Impossible match

Sanders led the preliminary exit poll of 1510 respondents 52.1-45.9% (787-693). He led the adjusted exit poll (matched to the recorded vote) of 1601 respondents by 49.8-48.3% (797-773). But the recorded share was IMPOSSIBLE. The proof is self-explanatory: How could Clinton win 80 and Sanders just 10 of the final 91 exit poll respondents? Based on the two-party preliminary share (53.16-46.84%) and 3.27% margin of error, Sanders had a 97.1% win probability.

Sanders did better than his recorded vote in the primary. Sanders won in 73 of 83 counties with 56% of the vote. He won the preliminary exit poll by 52.1-45.9%, a 97% win probability. Clinton won urban counties Wayne and Oakland with approximately 55% of the vote.

Preliminary Exit Poll - 1510 respondents

	Pct	Clinton	Sanders	Other
Men	0.45	0.42	0.56	0.02
Women	0.55	0.49	0.49	0.02
	100%	45.9%	52.2%	2.0%

CNN Adjusted Exit Poll - 1601 respondents

	Pct	Clinton	Sanders	Other
Men	0.45	0.44	0.55	0.02
Women	0.55	0.51	0.45	0.03
Total	100%	47.9%	49.5%	2.6%

	Resp.	Clinton	Sanders	Other
Adjusted	1601	773	797	30
Unadjusted	1510	693	787	29
Change	91	80	10	1

There were multiple indications of fraud: Cumulative vote shares, preliminary exit poll, absentee vote anomalies and other anecdotal information. Fraud abounds in heavily populated urban and suburban locations. Absentee Votes (AV) differed substantially from the overall county vote results. Generally absentee voting is a close match to the precincts. The Democrats had an estimated 237,000 AV. Approximately 177,750 (76%) voted for Clinton and 59,250 for Sanders. One would expect that Sanders and Clinton would nearly split AV.

Clinton had 75% of approximately 240,000 absentee votes and 51.2% of approximately 700,000 votes cast on ES&S Mod 100 machines. The percentages are highly suspect. Some have suggested that the reason Clinton won absentees by 50% is that they are typically older voters who supported Hillary. But Clinton won 60% of 45+ voters in the adjusted final exit poll. Clinton probably had less than 60%. So much for the age issue.

Sanders had 1) 56% at the 600,000 Cumulative vote share mark, 2) 54% of approximately 500,000 votes cast on AccuVote and Sequoia voting machines and 3) led 52.1-45.9% in the unadjusted exit poll. In the CVS analysis, Sanders had approximately 56% at the 600,000 mark. Notice the abrupt change to straight lines at the 600,000 vote mark. They represent the largest counties (Wayne and Oakland which used ES&S optical scanners exclusively.

Sanders' county vote shares were negatively correlated to machine type. The ES&S Model 100 correlation was -0.68. The bigger the county the lower Sanders' vote share.

Wayne and Oakland counties used ES&S Model 100 optical scanners. Macomb used both ES&S and Premier/Diebold/Dominion AccuVote optical scanners.

Cumulative Vote Shares by County Machine Type

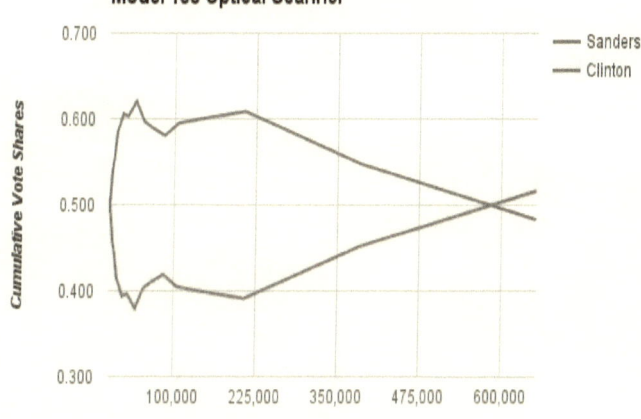

MI Primary Cumulative Vote Shares: ES&S Model 100 Optical Scanner

Cumulative Votes -smallest to largest counties

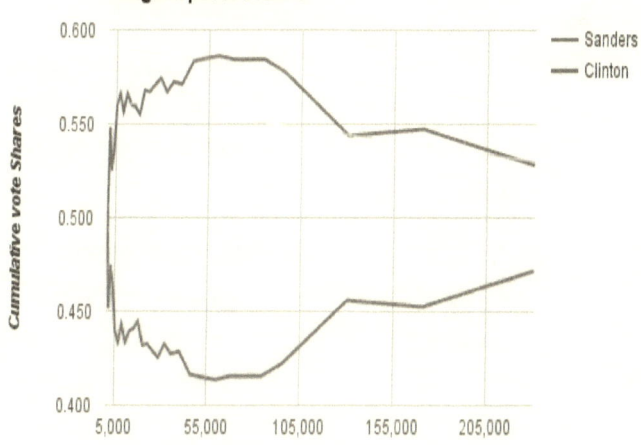

MI Primary Cumulative Vote Shares: Optech Insight Optical Scanner

Cumulative Votes- smallest to largest counties

Illinois

Clinton was declared the winner of the Illinois primary by 50.5 -
48.7% but Dr. Laura Chamberlain, spokesperson for Who's
Counting, told the Chicago Elections Board: *"The auditors, the
people that are doing the hand tallies of the votes, would miss votes,
would correct their tallies, erase their tallies, to fit the prescribed,
recommended, official results that the board of elections has right on
their tally sheets."*

The Chicago Board of Elections proved fraud in an audit to check
voting machines. It was not an official recount and will not change
the election outcome. A CBOE employee recounting an early voting
machine corrected the tally to square with the electoral result, even
though the hand-count was off by 70 votes in favor of Clinton.

Dr. Chamberlain saw an auditor intentionally remove 21 votes from
Bernie Sanders and add 49 votes to Hillary Clinton. Other observers
testified that they witnessed election officials counting ballots up to
the number on the machine read-out and ignored additional ballots
beyond that number. *The Chicago Board of Elections has confirmed
the existence of video evidence showing voter machines erasing
votes.*

Citizens from the watchdog group *Who's Counting* witnessed
Chicago officials tampering with the totals from paper ballot hand-
count audits of optical scan voting machines to force the paper ballot
totals to match the voting machines. The audits witnessed by the
group provide a random snapshot of the machine audits in Illinois.

Guidelines published by the US Department of Justice, "Federal
Prosecution of Election Offenses," defines "election fraud" as
"conduct intended to corrupt" the process by which ballots are

obtained, marked, or tabulated, election results are canvassed and certified, or by which voters are registered.

In all paper trail voting systems, the paper ballots are considered the authoritative record of the vote. The optical scan machines used in Chicago are similar to those used in thousands of jurisdictions across the country.

Jon Barnard, an Illinois county state's attorney, asked a judge to allow late votes for voters who could not vote in the primary because polling stations ran out of ballots. In an interview with US Uncut, Barnard said the votes could have altered the outcome between Sanders and Clinton. A judge granted the request, but the decision was reversed in appellate court after the state attorney general, Lisa Madigan, a Clinton supporter, requested that the order be blocked.

According to the DOJ, understaffing polling stations or ballot snafus do not rise to the level of criminal conduct, but altering true vote totals does.

Chicago election law requires a random 5% audit of ballots in order to verify that the hand counted tally of the ballots scanned by a machine matches the totals displayed by that machine. According to Illinois law, irregularities found in an audit, are supposed to trigger additional audits beyond the initial 5%. Sanders supporters are gearing up for a lawsuit based on the testimony of *Who's Counting*.

March 15

In the five unadjusted exit polls there were 7,220 respondents. Clinton led by 53.2-44.7%. In the final adjusted polls , there were 7979 respondents (759 additional). She led the final adjusted polls (which were matched to the recorded vote) by 55.6-42.4%.Clinton had 586 (77.2%) of the FINAL 759 respondents, or 21.9% above her unadjusted share. Sanders had 20% (24.7% below his unadjusted share).

EXIT POLLS VERSUS REPORTED VOTE COUNT - 2016 PRIMARIES

Democratic Party	CNN EXIT POLLS [1]					NYT REPORTED VOTE COUNT [2]				
	CLINTON	SANDERS	MARGIN CLINTON-SANDERS	NUMBER RESPONDENTS	MoE [3] ON THE DIFFERENCE	CLINTON	SANDERS	MARGIN CLINTON-SANDERS	DISCREPANCY IN FAVOR OF CLINTON	DISCREPANCY GREATER THAN EP MoE
NORTH CAROLINA	53.8%	41.7%	12.1%	1,744	4.55%	54.60%	40.80%	13.8%	1.7%	
FLORIDA	63.7%	35.9%	27.9%	1,632	4.65%	64.50%	33.30%	31.2%	3.4%	
ILLINOIS	48.4%	50.7%	-2.3%	1,341	5.33%	50.46%	48.72%	1.7%	4.1%	
MISSOURI	47.4%	51.1%	-3.7%	831	6.75%	49.60%	49.40%	0.2%	3.9%	
OHIO	51.4%	47.6%	3.8%	1,670	4.77%	56.50%	42.70%	13.8%	10.0%	5.2%

[1] Exit polls published by CNN shortly after the closing of polls for the state.
[2] New York Times reported 99% vote count   http://www.nytimes.com/elections/results
[3] Note that the Margin of Error (MoE) is for the differences between the two candidates (at 95% CI). This MoE is about double the usual MoE for each candidate. MoE calculated according to: Franklin, C. The 'Margin of Error' for Differences in Polls. University of Wisconsin, Madison, Wisconsin. October 2002, revised February 2007. Available at:
https://abcnews.go.com/images/PollingUnit/MOEFranklin.pdf

Wyoming Caucus

Bernie was a 56-44% winner, but Hillary won 11 of 18 delegates! In 12 counties, 54% of Clinton's votes were surrogates (mail-in), representing 74% of the delegates compared to 27% of Sander's votes. Contrast this to the Nebraska caucus, where 20% of Clinton's votes were mail-in.

CNN reported: "*A Clinton campaign aide said their 'secret sauce' in Wyoming was the state's onerous vote-by-mail rules that required anyone voting by mail to have voted as a Democrat in the 2014 midterms.*" But there is no evidence of such a rule. The aide was not named.

Utah apparently had a fair election. Note the parallel CVS lines representing Sanders and Clinton vote shares. Compare to Missouri. Clinton's share grew sharply in the largest urban areas in St. Louis and Kansas City.

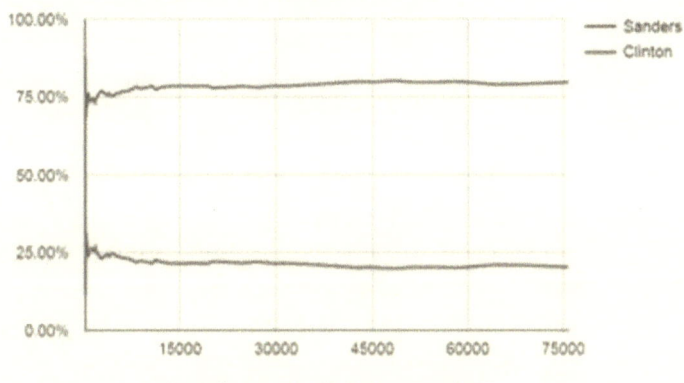

Cumulative votes (smallest to largest precincts)

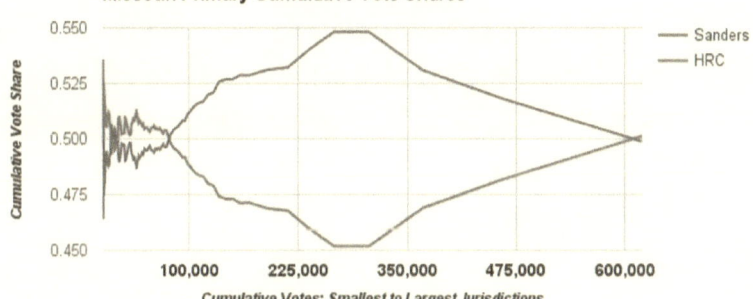

Cumulative Votes: Smallest to Largest Jurisdictions

Arizona

Arizona is the latest poster child of election fraud, along with Florida 2000 and Ohio 2004. Sanders won Utah (a bordering state) and Idaho primaries with nearly 80% of the vote. But he lost in Arizona by 60-38%. Who believes it?

The National Exit Pool (NEP) of six major media conglomerates funds exit pollster Edison Research. The NEP decided not to poll AZ. It's as if they knew they would have to match the unadjusted poll to a bogus recorded vote; the massive discrepancies would be too obvious. But the networks called it for Hillary with less than 1% of the votes in. How did they call the state without an exit poll?

Luckily the Yavapai County Daily Courier did an exit poll – and Bernie led by 63-37%. Hillary won the county by 54-43% - an impossible 37% difference in margin. But the evidence of fraud goes much further than this one poll.

In Yavapai County, **2/3 of the voters who came at the polls were not counted** because the DNC system registered them as independents.
http://usuncut.com/politics/5-examples-voter-suppression-arizona-primary/).

An Election Day Technician in Yavapai County voting center 5 on Tuesday, told US Uncut that roughly two thirds of voters who came to her precinct had been mistakenly identified as independent by the election software. All of those voters were subsequently forced to cast a provisional ballot.

The probability of the 5.8% difference in voter turnout between 14 AZ counties (56.0%) and Maricopa (50.2%) is approximately 1 in 13,000). The data is from the Arizona Secretary of State:

http://apps.azsos.gov/election/2016/PPE/Results/PPE2016Results.ht
m#

Pima County (Tucson): Hillary led VBM by 59.9-38.2%. But Sanders led the precinct vote by 59.1-39.6% at 11:20. There were 98,303 VBM but just 25,697 precinct votes. The voting machines used were ES&S (Optiscan); Premier Accuvote (Optiscan)

Maricopa County (Phoenix): At 8pm HRC led VBM by 61.5-36.1% of 114,286 votes. Sanders led the 32,959 precinct votes by 60.3-38.8%. The voting machines used were the AVC Edge (DRE); Optech Insight (Optiscan); Optech 400C (Optiscan). Voters had to stand on line to vote and incensed that the primary was been called for Hillary Clinton. Approximately 1.3 million voters who reportedly would have voted for Sanders were disenfranchised. Approximately 70% of voters were turned away because they were registered independents – and Bernie won a solid majority of them.

The *Arizona Republic* reported that Maricopa County reduced the number of polling places from more than 200 in the 2012 presidential election to 60. Arizona law effectively disenfranchises 36 percent of registered voters. Registered Democrats who had voted in primaries before were told that they were not on the Democratic voting lists. Others who switched their party were told they were not on the list – but could vote on a provisional ballot.

At 2:45 AM ET, Sanders was leading Clinton in Election Day voting in Arizona 50.2% to 49.8%, with just under 75,000 votes (about 17.3% of all Election Day votes) counted. The media called the election for Clinton with less than 1% of the vote counted and thousands waiting in line to vote.

Voters had to stand on line to vote and incensed that the primary was been called for Hillary Clinton. Approximately 1.3 million voters who reportedly would have voted for Sanders were disenfranchised. Approximately 70% of voters were turned away because they were registered independents – and Bernie won a solid majority of them.

The *Arizona Republic* reported that Maricopa County reduced the number of polling places from more than 200 in the 2012 presidential election to 60. Arizona law effectively disenfranchises 36 percent of registered voters. Registered Democrats who had voted in primaries before were told that they were not on the Democratic voting lists. Others who switched their party were told they were not on the list – but could vote on a provisional ballot.

At 2:45 AM ET, Sanders was leading Clinton in Election Day voting in Arizona 50.2% to 49.8%, with just under 75,000 votes (about 17.3% of all Election Day votes) counted. The media called the election for Clinton with less than 1% of the vote counted and thousands waiting in line to vote.

Four hours after polling stations closed, hundreds of people were still waiting in line: 37% (1.219 million) of registered voters declared as independents; 34% (1.115 million) as Republicans; and 28% (932,722) as Democrats. Sanders has won a vast majority of independents in every state.

Bomb threats prevented many voters from getting the help they needed: Two hours after polls closed in Arizona, officials there had counted only 54,000 of the estimated 431,000 (12% of Election Day ballots.

Maricopa (Phoenix) is the largest of 15 AZ counties with nearly 60% of the vote. Pima County (Tucson) is second with 16%. In the 2008 primary, Maricopa turnout was 54.3%. It was 47.2% in the other counties. In 2016, 14 counties had higher turnout rates than in 2008. The 4.1% decline in Maricopa 2016 turnout (50.2%) from 2008 is counter-intuitive. Voter turnout in the other 14 AZ counties increased 8.8% to 56.0%. Based on the trend, Maricopa should have had an approximate 63.1% (54.3%+8.8%) turnout. Approximately 160,000 votes were suppressed. The probability of the 12.9% difference between Maricopa's projected and actual turnout is 1 in 90 trillion. The probability of the 5.8% difference in turnout between 14 counties and Maricopa is 1 in 600,000.

County	2016 Registration	Votes	Turnout	2008 Turnout	Chg
Maricopa	1,238,508	621,976	50.2%	54.3%	-4.1%
Pima	327,699	202,934	61.9%	52.4%	9.5%
Yavapai	82,057	56,454	68.8%	51.6%	17.2%
Pinal	98,112	52,221	53.2%	46.1%	7.1%
Mohave	65,409	33,552	51.3%	43.2%	8.1%
Cochise	45,952	24,310	52.9%	43.5%	9.4%
Coconino	45,385	26,278	57.9%	49.3%	8.6%
Yuma	43,937	20,105	45.8%	39.3%	6.4%
Navajo	42,254	18,066	42.8%	37.3%	5.5%
Gila	20,503	11,698	57.1%	50.9%	6.1%
Apache	34,635	11,360	32.8%	28.1%	4.7%
Santa Cruz	15,707	6,098	38.8%	33.8%	5.0%
Graham	13,073	5,966	45.6%	38.3%	7.4%
La Paz	5,592	2,004	35.8%	42.3%	-6.5%
Greenlee	3,131	1,557	49.7%	44.1%	5.6%
Total	2,081,954	1,094,579	52.6%	51.3%	1.3%

Wisconsin

Bernie Sanders had 563,127 votes (56.5%) and Hillary Clinton 429.738 (43.1%). At 4pm, the exit poll indicated that Sanders had 68% of white vote. Whites comprise 88% of WI voters. Assuming Sanders had just 40% of the non-white vote, he won the election by an estimated 64.6-35.4% (2-party).

The final adjusted exit poll was forced to match the recorded vote. It indicates that whites comprised 83% of the vote and Sanders had just 59%. Blacks comprised 10% and Sanders had 31%. These numbers are not plausible. A pre-election poll from Public Policy Polling (PPP) indicated that Sanders was winning black voters by 51-40%.

The exit poll shows that 7% of voters were Latino (3%), Asian (2%), Other (2%). According to the pollsters, the vote shares are NA. How is that? The pollsters could have combined the 7% as Other Non-whites. Without this information, we cannot calculate the total recorded vote shares. The abbreviated totals have Sanders winning by 52.1-40.1%. The 12% margin is close to the official margin.

The final adjusted CNN WI Exit Poll indicates that whites comprised 83% of the electorate (Sanders had 59%). The probability of the 9% decline from 68% to 59% is 1 in 4000. But Census tables showed that whites comprise 92% of the Wisconsin electorate. Assume 88% were whites. Blacks comprised 10% of the vote. If Sanders had 31% of non-whites, he won WI by 63.6-36.4%.Why the 20% decline in Sanders 51% pre-election poll share of blacks and 9% decline in Sanders 68% exit poll share of whites? Seven percent were Latino (3%).

Race	Pct	Sanders	Clinton
White	88.0%	59.0%	41.0%
Non-white	12.0%	31.0%	69.0%
TOTAL	100.0%	55.6%	44.4%

5pm	Pct	Sanders	Clinton
White	88.0%	68.0%	32.0%
Non-white	12.0%	31.0%	69.0%
TOTAL	100.0%	63.6%	36.4%
	Recorded	56.5%	43.5%
	Adjusted	55.6%	44.4%

		% White		
Sanders	59.0%	64.0%	68.0%	72.0%
%Non-white		Sanders %		
51.0%	58.0%	62.4%	66.0%	69.5%
40.0%	56.7%	61.1%	64.6%	68.2%
35.0%	56.1%	60.5%	64.0%	67.6%
31.0%	55.6%	60.0%	63.6%	67.1%

New York

Momentum was on Bernie's side. He had just won a solid victory in Wisconsin. Now he was coming home. A Brooklyn native, he was drawing great crowds. The following entertainers gave speeches on his behalf: Harry Belafonte, Tim Robbins, Susan Sarandon, Mark Ruffalo, Spike Lee, Rosario Dawson.

NYC was a natural for Bernie, despite the fact that Hillary Clinton was a senator for eight years. But it was Arizona all over again. Thousands of voters reported their registrations were changed or dropped. Only 22% of 8 million registered voters turned out. Clinton won by 57.9-42.1%.

The UNADJUSTED exit poll indicated a close race. Hillary led by just 52-48%, an 11.8% discrepancy from the recorded vote. There were 1391 respondents and a 2.6% exit poll Margin of Error. Clinton led by 62-38% with 33% of precincts reporting.

At 9:03 pm, there were 1307 respondents. Clinton led the count by 680-627 (52.0-48.0%). With just 84 additional respondents (1391 total), Clinton's lead increased to 802-589 (57.7-42.3%). She had 122 additional respondents and Sanders had 38 fewer.

How can Clinton gain 122 of 84 respondents? How can Sanders' total drop? They can't. It is mathematically impossible. Therefore the final vote has to be impossible as well. The exit poll was forced to match the recorded vote with impossible adjustments.

In 2014, the NY voter registration split was 49D-24R-27I. The split was 85D-15I in the exit poll, which (as always) was forced to match the 57.9-42.1% recorded vote. Assuming primary voting was proportional to registration, the split would have been 65D-35I and the race would have been a tie. If Clinton had 58% of Democrats, Sanders won the election by 52.5-47.5%.

How did the pollsters adjust Sanders 48% share in the NY primary at 9pm (1307 respondents) to 42.1% at the final (1391 respondents). This indicates that an equivalent of 107,000 votes were flipped from Bernie to Clinton.

The pollsters had to increase the percentage of women voters by 1%, Clinton's share of men by 5% and her share of women by 6%. The 125 increase in Clinton's respondents among the final 84 exit poll respondents is obviously impossible. That is proof of Election Fraud in the NY Primary.

Note: the exit poll does not include approximately 400,000 disenfranchised voters (120,000 in Brooklyn).

9pm UNADJUSTED EXIT POLL MoE: 2.71%

	Total	Clinton	Sanders	Margin
Votes (000)	1790	930	860	70
Respondents	1307	680	627	63
Exit Poll	100%	52.0%	48.0%	4.0%

1307 respondents (CNN)

Gender	Pct	Clinton	Sanders	Margin
Men	42%	45%	55%	-10%
Women	58%	57%	43%	14%
Total	100%	52.0%	48.0%	4.0%

ADJUSTED EXIT POLL (match recorded vote)

Recorded	Total	Clinton	Sanders	Margin
Votes (000)	1790	1037	753	284
Respondents	1391	805	586	219
Adj Exit Poll	100%	57.9%	42.1%	15.8%

1391 respondents (CNN)

Gender	Pct	Clinton	Sanders	Margin
Men	41%	50%	50%	0%
Women	59%	63%	37%	26%
Total	100%	57.7%	42.3%	15.3%

NY True Vote Estimate

Given Sanders' 48% unadjusted exit poll, he must have won the primary due to vote suppression. Assuming 5% of registered voters (400,000) were disenfranchised and Sanders had 70%, then he won NY with 52.0%.

TV = 52% = 48% Voted + 70% Disenfranchised
= 48%* 1790 + 70% * 400 = 860+280
= 1140 / 2190

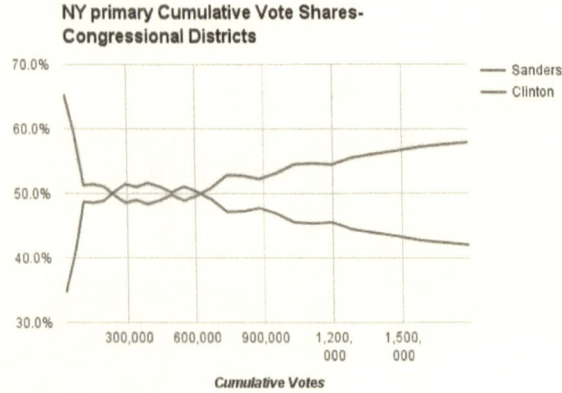

NY primary Cumulative Vote Shares-
Congressional Districts

Sensitivity Analysis

Sanders Share of Disenfranchised

Share of Exit Poll	60.0%	65.0%	70.0%	75.0%	80.0%
Sanders					
50.0%	52.7%	53.6%	54.6%	55.5%	56.4%
49.0%	51.9%	52.8%	53.7%	54.6%	55.6%
48.0%	51.1%	52.0%	52.0%	53.8%	54.7%
47.0%	50.3%	51.2%	52.1%	53.0%	53.9%
46.0%	49.5%	50.4%	51.3%	52.2%	53.1%

New York Adjusted Exit Poll

		Clinton	Sanders	Margin		Clinton	Sanders	Margin
Adj Exit Poll Resp	1391	57.93%	42.07%	15.87%	Unadj. Exit poll	51.96%	48.04%	3.92%
Votes (000)	1790	1037	753	284	1307 Resp	930	860	70
Gender	Mix	Clinton	Sanders	Margin	Mix	Clinton	Sanders	Margin
Men	41%	50%	50%	0%	42%	45%	55%	-10%
Women	59%	63%	37%	26%	58%	57%	43%	14%
Total	100%	57.67%	42.33%	15.34%	100%	51.96%	48.04%	3.92%

Age	Mix	Clinton	Sanders	Margin	Mix	Clinton	Sanders	Margin
18-29	18%	35%	65%	-30%	17%	28%	72%	-44%
30-44	24%	53%	47%	6%	24%	46%	54%	-8%
45-64	39%	63%	37%	26%	39%	57%	43%	14%
65+	19%	73%	27%	46%	20%	70%	30%	40%
Total	100%	57.46%	42.54%	14.92%	100%	52.03%	47.97%	4.06%

Race	Mix	Clinton	Sanders	Margin	Mix	Clinton	Sanders	Margin
white	59%	50%	50%	0%	59%	45%	54%	-9%
black	22%	75%	25%	50%	22%	71%	28%	43%
latino	14%	64%	36%	28%	14%	59%	41%	18%
asian	2%	n/a	n/a	n/a	2%	n/a	n/a	n/a
other	3%	n/a	n/a	n/a	3%	n/a	n/a	n/a
Total	100%	54.96%	45.04%	9.92%	100%	50.43%	43.76%	6.67%

Party ID	Mix	Clinton	Sanders	Margin	Mix	Clinton	Sanders	Margin
Democrats	83%	62%	38%	24%	83%	57%	43%	14%
Republicans	3%	n/a	n/a		3%	n/a	n/a	n/a
Independents	14%	28%	72%	-44%	14%	22%	78%	-56%
Total	100%	55.38%	44.62%	10.76%	100%	50.39%	49.61%	0.78%

Philosophy	Mix	Clinton	Sanders	Margin	Mix	Clinton	Sanders	Margin
Very liberal	29%	44%	56%	-12%	29%	47%	53%	-6%
Liberal	37%	59%	41%	18%	37%	59%	41%	18%
Moderate	29%	67%	33%	34%	29%	62%	37%	25%
Conservative	5%	n/a	n/a	n/a	5%	na	na	n/a
Total	100%	54.02%	45.98%	8.04%	100%	53.44%	46.56%	6.88%

Area	Mix	Clinton	Sanders	Margin	Mix	Clinton	Sanders	Margin
Urban	64%	62%	38%	24%	55%	55%	44%	11%
Suburban	31%	51%	49%	2%	38%	48%	51%	-3%
Rural	6%	n/a	n/a		7%	48%	52%	-4%
Total	101%	55.49%	44.51%	10.98%	100%	51.85%	47.22%	4.63%

Region	Mix	Clinton	Sanders	Margin	Mix	Clinton	Sanders	Margin
New York City	52%	63%	37%	26%	42%	55%	45%	10%
Urban Upstate	14%	50%	50%	0%	17%	52%	48%	4%
Rural Upstate	9%	42%	58%	-16%	12%	38%	62%	-24%
Total	100%	57.72%	42.28%	15.44%	100%	51.94%	48.06%	3.88%

Louisiana

This is from *Voting irregularities linked to companies that donated to the Clinton Foundation.* by **Axel Geijsel**, Tilburg University & **Rodolfo Cortes Barragan**, Stanford University. It illustrates the use of Cumulative Vote shares in detecting fraud.

There were no exit polls in Louisiana.

Louisiana is a state with 100% electronic voting, Sen. Sanders is the only candidate in either party who was at an overwhelming disadvantage in larger precincts. This does not simply reflect an urban vs. rural distinction. There are large precincts in small towns and small precincts in big cities.

The authors did not observe any candidate gaining a larger share of the vote in larger Republican precincts (the lines were relatively stable as precinct size increased).

However, they observed that Hillary Clinton's share of the votes kept increasing (up to 25%). This statistical abnormality was seen in almost every parish (county), but did not appear for the Republican primary

Why would voters in larger precincts favor one candidate over the other by such a wide margin? The authors were unable to come up with a reasonable psychological or sociological reason that would apply *only* to voters in the Democratic primary.

Therefore, the data <u>suggests</u> that Clinton won in counties and in states where Clinton Foundation donors are responsible for the voting machines.

http://thebernreport.com/study-shows-voting-irregularities-linked-to-companies-that-donated-to-the-clinton-foundation/

Kentucky

Clinton won by 2,000 of 413,000 votes: 46.8-46.3%

At one point, all Pike County data represented all zeroes in the vote totals. Later, 20 percent of the total votes were missing and Clinton gained the lead. *WKYT* reported that the AP had actually "erased all votes from Pike County" which put Clinton back up by over 4,000. The Pike County Clerk's Office said that there was an issue with one of their card readers, and it ended up causing them to have a delay in posting their numbers.Election fraud was reported in 31 counties.

There were at least 76 calls to the hotline of the Office of the Kentucky Attorney General, Andy Beshear. According to Kentucky news station WSAZ, *'Complaints included procedural and legal questions, voter assistance, [issues with] voting machines, voter identification, residency, election officials, electioneering, poll disruption and vote buying.*

Jefferson is the largest county in KY and Clinton is the establishment candidate. Clinton's cumulative vote share increased by 7.4% (55.9% to 63.3%) after 85% of smaller precincts were counted!

Figure 1

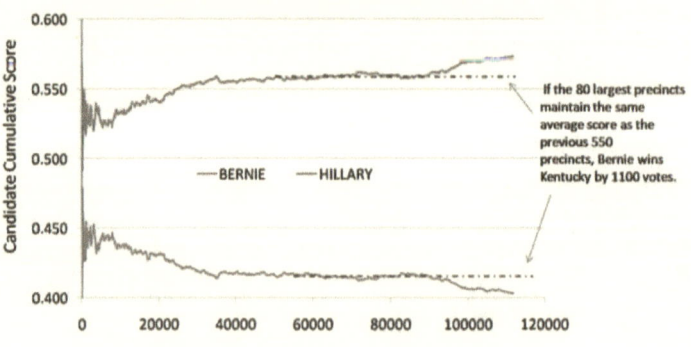

Jefferson County Kentucky CVS by Ascending Precinct Size

Miraculously, Hillary's average precinct score jumps from 55.9 to 63.3% (7.4%) the last 80 precincts to catapult her to victory by 1,924 votes.

If the 80 largest precincts maintain the same average score as the previous 550 precincts, Bernie wins Kentucky by 1100 votes.

—BERNIE   —HILLARY

Cumulative Total Votes ordered by Ascending Precinct Size

Oregon

Sanders won 56-44%. He had 53% at the 60% mark and 56% at 96%. Therefore he had 67% of the 36% late votes. Late Votes = 67.2% = (0.56-0.53*0.6)/0.36. In 2014, the voter registration mix was Dem 37.8-Rep 29.9-Ind 32.3. Assuming Independents could have voted in the primary, Sanders would have won by approximately 65-35% which agrees with the 67% calculated above.

	Sanders	Clinton	Total
Oregon Star	341,472	261,145	602,617
	56.66%	43.34%	100.00%
AP	320,746	251,739	572,485
	56.03%	43.97%	100.00%
	Votes in	Sanders	Clinton
	60%	53%	47%
	96%	56%	44%
Change	36%	67.2%	32.8%

OR Registration	2014	Adjusted	Sanders	Clinton
Dem (recorded)	37.80%	53.9%	56.0%	44.0%
Independent	32.30%	46.1%	75.0%	25.0%
Adjusted share	70.10%	100.0%	64.8%	35.2%
Estimated	2016			
Dem (recorded)	35.00%	46.7%	56.0%	44.0%
Independent	40.00%	53.3%	75.0%	25.0%
Adjusted share	75.00%	100.0%	66.1%	33.9%
Change			67.2%	32.8%

Connecticut

Clinton won the primary by 18,000 votes (51.8-46.4%). There was just a 1.4% exit poll discrepancy while NY had an 11.8% discrepancy. There were 1234 total exit poll respondents. But according to ABC News, Sanders was leading the preliminary exit poll by 55-40%. Assuming 800 respondents at 4:30, the poll had a 4.5% margin of error. For Clinton's share to increase by 12% with just 434 additional respondents is virtually impossible.

Adjusted exit poll   **Preliminary exit poll**

Final	Pct	Clinton	Sanders	Other	Pct	Clinton	Sanders	Other
Men	39%	43%	**55%**	2%	39%	25%	**70%**	5%
women	61%	**55%**	41%	4%	61%	**50%**	**46%**	4%
	Total	**50.32%**	**46.46%**	**3.22%**	**Total**	**40.25%**	**55.36%**	**4.39%**
	2-party	51.99%	48.01%		2-party	**42.10%**	**57.90%**	
	Recorded	51.80%	46.40%	1.80%	Recorded	51.80%	46.40%	1.80%
	Diff	**-1.48%**	**0.06%**	**1.42%**	**Diff**	**-11.55%**	**8.96%**	**2.59%**
Votes	328,395	170,075	152,410	5,910	328,395	132,179	181,799	14,417
		Discrepancy 5.53%				Discrepancy -20.51%		

Connecticut Democratic Primary

| | Hillary Clinton | 52% | 170,075 |
| | Bernie Sanders | 46% | 152,410 |

Exit Poll

ⓐNEWS EXIT POLL 2016
CONNECTICUT PRIMARY PRELIMINARY EXIT POLL DATA

| SANDERS | | 55% |
| CLINTON | | 40% |

#ForThePeople
@BernieVolunteer

Follow

Exit poll @ABC for #CT show Bernie winning 55%. But election results show 46%. How?What's the Purpose of Exit polls?
6.08 PM - 12 May 2016

↩ ⇄ 219 ♥ 211

Puerto Rico

Puerto Rican officials expected 700,000 people to vote in the 2016 Democratic primary. The Democratic Party announced that more than 1,500 polling places would be available for the primary. A few weeks later, they cut the number to just over 430. There were more than 2300 polling places in the 2008 primary,

Many voters had to visit two locations to cast ballots in the presidential primary and the local primaries. Puerto Rico voter turnout has traditionally been very high. Supporters of Sen. Bernie Sanders (I-VT) called it a "fix", drawing parallels to Arizona's primary.

Just 60,000 votes were cast in the primary. The Puerto Rico Democratic Party accused the *Sanders campaign* of requesting fewer polling places.

Sanders' issued the following statement on long lines at polling places in Puerto Rico's Democratic Party presidential primary election:

"Some Puerto Rico Democratic officials are claiming that the Sanders campaign requested fewer polling places in today's primary contest. That's completely false. The opposite is true.

In emails with the party, Sanders' staff asked the party to maintain the 1,500 plus presidential primary locations promised by the Puerto Rico Democratic Party in testimony before the DNC in April, *when the party was asking to have its caucus changed to a primary. They cannot blame their shoddy running of the primary on our campaign. This is just one example of irregularities going on in Puerto Rico voting today. We are the campaign that has been fighting to increase voter participation."*

California

Poll workers indicated that at least hundreds of thousands of voters who were supposed to have been eligible to vote in the Democratic primary were told they would have to vote provisional ballots. Registered voters' names had been removed from the rolls. They had been marked as vote by mail - but the voters did not receive the ballots in the mail. Virtually all who were forced to vote provisional ballots were Bernie Sanders supporters.

Poll workers in Los Angeles and Orange County reported that Bernie won the electronic votes in their precincts by well over a 2 to 1 margin, the opposite of the vote count. New voters were overwhelmingly planning to vote for Bernie. Of the NPP (no party preference) voters, the vast majority were Sanders supporters.

The Sanders campaign used a program *Minivan* for canvassing. In Arizona, Sanders poll workers were told on the last day before the election that it was known that the program had been hacked and that people would be using paper canvassing sheets. Almost all the canvassing had already been done in Arizona. The Sanders volunteers who canvassed voters input the following to *Minivan*: "Strong Sanders," "Leaning Sanders," "Strong Clinton", "Leaning Clinton," or "Undecided". This data was useful for disenfranchising voters in California.

An instructional video for poll workers told them to give provisional ballots to NPP voters, official conduct that would have been illegal in California. AP joined in the effort to try to fix the election by calling the nomination for Clinton the night before the election even though Clinton would not have enough pledged delegates to be the nominee. This appears to have been part of the overall attempt to suppress the vote. Sanders has repeatedly pointed out, *"If there is a large turnout we will win. If there is a very large turnout we will win huge. If there is a low turnout, we will lose."*

Turnout was very high. Without suppression, Sanders would have won. Polling place workers told of Sanders winning by more than a 2 to 1 margin. On Election Day, Clinton led Sanders 56.8-43.2% in machine-counted mail-in ballots. Sanders leads in hand-counted mail-ins by 51.1-48.9% (391,012-374,839 votes). As usual, votes were flipped on maliciously-coded voting machines and central tabulators. Nearly 15% of Sanders' votes were flipped to Clinton. Sanders hand-counted share exceeded his machine-counted share in EVERY county. The probability of this occurrence is absolute ZERO.

Election Justice USA, a voter advocacy non-profit organization, claims that a Capitol Weekly early-voter exit poll conducted across the state of California yielded a 23 percent discrepancy in Los Angeles vote-by-mail ballots compared to the actual results. During the polling of the early round of mail-in voters, Hillary Clinton had a lead over Bernie Sanders in the Los Angeles area that was less than 10 percent.

According to EJ USA, *"The discrepancy cannot be easily explained by demographic factors: the results of the Capitol Weekly exit poll were weighted by age and race. Moreover, the exit poll had 21,000 respondents, and was praised–prior to election night–by mainstream elections journalists, including Nate Cohn of the New York Times. While no exit poll can prove fraud, a significant exit polling discrepancy such as this constitutes cause for alarm, especially one of this magnitude. It's also sufficient cause for immediate action: voters should bring pressure to bear on officials and demand an expanded hand audit."*

BBC reporter, author and election fraud expert Greg Palast Nightline used his footage in covering the story. This is from Greg's article, "How California is being stolen from Sanders right now." "As I've previously reported, provisional ballots are "placebo" ballots that let you feel like you've voted, but you haven't. Provisional ballots are generally discarded."

Simple CA Vote share Model

There was no exit poll, so let's assume the following.
a) Party-ID: 57% Independents vs. 43% Democrats
b) Sanders won 70% of Independents

Clinton needed an implausible 85% of Democrats to match her
53.5% recorded share.

Party-ID.... Pct ... ...Sanders....Clinton
IND......... 57.0%...... 70.0%..... 30.0%
DEM........ 43.0%......15.3%..... 84.7%
Total.......100.0%...... 46.5%..... 53.5%
Recorded............... 46.5%..... 53.5%

Sensitivity Analysis

.... Sanders % Independents				
Sanders........ 55%	60%	70%	75%	80%
% DEM............. Sanders Vote share				
45%............. 51%	54%	59%	62%	65%
40%............. 49%	51%	57%	60%	63%
35%............. 46%	49%	55%	58%	61%
30%............. 44%	47%	53%	56%	59%
25%............. 42%	45%	51%	54%	56%

 A Cumulative Vote Share (CVS) analysis of California counties,
sorted from smallest to largest, confirms the likelihood of fraud. In
virtually every CVS analysis, the establishment candidate (Clinton)
gains vote share. One would intuitively expect that the more
progressive candidate (Sanders) would slightly gain cumulative vote
share in the largest (typically liberal) urban and suburban counties.
The fact that Sanders does well in smaller, (typically conservative)
counties, is further indication of voter suppression, ballot destruction
and vote flipping in larger counties.

J.T. Waldron in electionnightmares.com: After painstaking construction of spreadsheet data comparing batches of California 2016 Primary Election ballots counted from election day until now, elections expert John Brakey has found a pattern that is consistent with a technique that is aptly named the "strip, stack and hack" approach to election fraud.

Brakey believes California election officials, in conjunction with their vendors, managed to "strip" the vote by rendering people ineligible to use a regular ballot prior to the election, "stack" likely Clinton voters to be counted first on election day and "hack" the batch of votes to be counted later without an audit.

After more than 700,000 California voters were stripped from being counted in a timely manner when forced to vote on a provisional ballot, vote-by-mail ballots from likely Clinton voters were stacked into the piles to be counted first. This enabled the establishment to report a huge 26% election night lead by Hillary Clinton over Bernie Sanders, which would quietly be reduced to a still shrinking single digit lead as remaining ballots continue to be counted.

A San Diego County Registrar insider claims that hundreds of thousands of California Democratic primary provisional ballots were illegally destroyed in a covert shredding operation. A consignment of boxes was delivered to the San Diego Registrar's Office at 5600 Overland Ave in the morning and an "oversized shredding van" arrived minutes later and took the boxes away. The boxes were carried from the building to the vehicle by men she had never seen before wearing dark blue overalls. In addition, http://embols.com/2016/07/06/ballots-with-sanders-votes-covered-with-white-out-filmed-by-election-monitors-in-san-diego/

"Citizen election monitors in San Diego have captured film of ballots which have been tampered with, with white-out erasing only Sanders votes, sometimes with part of Bernie Sanders' first name obscured as well. In the film, a monitor reports that almost half the ballots in the box of ballots she witnessed had been so altered, always against Sanders.
The mainstream media has yet to report on the startling discovery.

After the Illinois Democratic primary in March, a citizens' watchdog group monitoring an audit of the votes says they witnessed vote totals being tampered with to benefit Hillary Clinton.

In other video captured by citizen reporters and election monitors in San Diego, an election official attempts to keep monitors away from the windows of a room where "provisional" ballots are being counted by officials, which are ballots which were cast mostly by independent voters in the primary. At one point an election monitor, a woman, is told by an official who identifies herself as "Karen Mayer," to keep her voice down, as she questions what officials through the glass in an off-limits room are doing in the back. The woman tells the official that "you guys are violating the election code, and I'm not going to shut up about it."

In a follow up interview of another official, "Charlie Loomis," the IT manager, the manager confirms that it is indeed white-out that can be seen on the ballots, and that the ballots are being "manipulated." The IT manager goes on to say that, as a San Diego official, he has no control over this, as the white-outs are a result of Democratic party rules on how the ballots, which are provisional ballots, must be processed. Mr. Loomis say he has "nothing to do with" those rules. Mr. Loomis did indicate, however, that after the white-out process, the ballots are "run through the scanner again."

According to Greg Palast, Bernie won CA by at least 100,000 votes.
https://www.washingtonpost.com/news/post-politics/wp/2016/06/27/still-sanders-activists-cling-to-hope-of-flipping-california/

"They said, with 100 percent of precincts reporting, Hillary Clinton has won by 400,000 votes," Palast said of the media. "Now, I want you to say this number with me: 1,959,900. That's the number of ballots that were not yet counted. How do you say an election's over when there are 2 million ballots left to count?"

According to Palast, those ballots had the potential to flip the election. Based on a call to the secretary of state's office, he estimated that all of the outstanding ballots were from "no party preference" voters; based on a pre-primary poll, he estimated a 40 percentage point margin for Sanders among those ballots.

"Bernie Sanders got at least 1.25 million votes from that pile," Palast said. "The good news is that Bernie won California. ... If you count every ballot, Sanders would win by 100,000."

J.T. Waldron writes at http://electionnightmares.com/archives/564

As John Brakey states, *"Elections are only as strong as their weakest link".*

Despite California counting only 65% of the ballots on Election Day, media outlets like Politico and The New York Times ceased from covering the rest of the count, which leaves its audience assuming a literal interpretation of "100% of the precincts reporting", but that statement does not mean all the votes are counted. It only means precinct ballots from all of the precincts have been counted, but there are many vote-by-mail and provisional ballots that have yet to be included in this total.

On election night, shortly after 8:00 PM, the first results were released and they were 99% vote-by-mail ballots. The numbers showed Hillary Clinton with a decisive lead over Bernie Sanders by 25.94% points. Clinton received 62.56% to Sanders 36.63% with 1.52 million vote-by-mail ballots.

By early the next morning, another 1.94 million ballots were counted. Clinton received 50.73% and Sanders got 48.47%, but those numbers are deceiving. On Election Day, 718,869 voters were forced to vote a provisional ballot which, in my estimate, are 80% Democratic voters with at least 60% going to Sanders. This would be enough to flip the 'precinct vote' to Sanders, who would get 52% over Clinton's new total of 47%. This spread more accurately reflects the pre-election polling numbers.

American Democracy and Election Integrity (ADEI)

The Institute and Election Justice USA decided to jointly sponsor an exit poll because Edison Media Research decided to cancel exit polls for the rest of the USA after attorney Cliff Arnebeck wrote a letter to Edison Research Media asking to see the unadjusted data. There was also an article by Tim Robbins questioning the exit polls that were showing dramatic differences between the exit poll totals and the election night results. At about that time, Democratic presidential candidate Bernie Sanders was showing a very distinct lead against Clinton in twelve states, which disappeared shortly after the polls closed. This suggested that electronic manipulation of the polls was taking place. We at the Institute decided to run an exit poll close to our area in California to try to give voters a better picture of the true election results for at least three counties in California.

ADEI conducted exit polls during the 2016 California presidential primary in three counties at twelve precincts. The polls were randomized and representative of the demographic data in the precinct area. The counties were Contra Costa, Santa Clara, and Alameda and four polling places were chosen in each county. The sample size was 3,321.

The official vote for these three counties show Sanders winning over Clinton 49.2% to 46.1%, a 3.1% margin. Unadjusted exit polls conducted by the Institute showed Sanders winning by 52.6-43.8%. The results were adjusted for demographic data and Sanders led 51.9- 44.4%. Older white men did not often agree to fill out the exit poll. They tended to be Trump, Johnson and, occasionally, Clinton supporters. Gary Johnson is the Libertarian candidate. So some votes for Trump, Johnson and Clinton were added proportionally to the exit poll results.

The Institute used the Senate race as a "benchmark" against the presidential race. This is done in all good polling where you pair a vote you are interested in, like the presidential candidate with the senatorial candidate. The ADEI exit poll results for both candidates Kamala Harris and Loretta Sanchez matched the official voting tally within the 2 percent margin of error.

A 2 percent difference in the margin of error is common in most exit polls and is not considered a fraction of election irregularities or fraud.

California primary early vote by mail exit poll

Election Justice USA asserts that a Capitol Weekly early-voter exit poll conducted across the state of California yielded a 23 percent discrepancy in Los Angeles vote-by-mail ballots compared to the actual results. During the polling of the early round of mail-in voters, Hillary Clinton had a lead over Bernie Sanders in the Los Angeles area that was less than 10 percent. Election Justice USA said that the discrepancy was significant enough to demand a hand audit of early mail-in ballots.

Landslide in Humboldt County

In California, just ONE county uses an Open Source System to audit and count votes. Could that be why Bernie had 71% of the 2-party vote in Humboldt County? It was his highest vote share in ALL 58 counties! The system is a deterrent to fraud. View the 58 California counties: Election Day and post-Election Day votes

Post-election gain in Sanders vote shares

Sanders	Votes	Election Day	July 7	Gain
CALIFORNIA	5,097,033	**43.63%**	**46.56%**	**2.93%**
7/5 update				
ALAMEDA	318,844	46.0%	51.7%	5.7%
ALPINE	250	54.0%	54.8%	0.8%
AMADOR	4,902	47.4%	48.7%	1.3%
BUTTE	31,505	59.6%	62.7%	3.1%
CALAVERAS	5,885	47.6%	49.5%	1.9%
COLUSA	1,644	47.2%	49.2%	2.0%
CONTRA COSTA*	181,195	40.2%	43.0%	2.8%
DEL NORTE	2,717	56.6%	58.8%	2.2%
EL DORADO	25,112	47.8%	49.7%	1.9%
FRESNO	80,099	39.7%	43.3%	3.6%
GLENN	1,914	49.8%	52.4%	2.6%
HUMBOLDT*	28,063	68.7%	71.0%	2.3%
IMPERIAL	14,954	32.2%	34.2%	2.0%
INYO	2,314	55.9%	56.7%	0.9%
KERN	52,180	41.4%	44.8%	3.4%
KINGS	7,019	39.4%	40.9%	1.5%
LAKE	9,183	52.9%	56.6%	3.7%
LASSEN	1,835	52.7%	55.7%	3.0%
LOS ANGELES	1,419,899	42.4%	45.1%	2.7%
MADERA	10,660	42.9%	45.5%	2.6%
MARIN	76,497	42.2%	43.4%	1.3%

Sanders	Votes	Election Day	July 7	Gain
*7/5 update				
MARIPOSA	2,457	52.2%	55.1%	3.0%
MENDOCINO	18,307	63.4%	67.0%	3.6%
MERCED	20,112	42.0%	46.1%	4.1%
MODOC	630	53.8%	55.4%	1.6%
MONO	1,837	54.8%	56.5%	1.7%
MONTEREY	55,803	43.0%	46.7%	3.8%
NAPA	25,265	39.3%	46.2%	6.9%
NEVADA *	21,202	60.2%	61.4%	1.2%
ORANGE	327,828	44.9%	47.7%	2.8%
PLACER*	46,165	42.5%	45.3%	2.8%
PLUMAS	2,686	55.0%	54.9%	-0.1%
RIVERSIDE *	198,444	39.4%	43.3%	3.9%
SACRAMENTO	199,326	42.6%	44.9%	2.3%
SAN BERNARDINO	173,782	42.1%	44.7%	2.6%
SAN BENITO	7,492	41.6%	45.1%	3.5%
SAN DIEGO *	415,371	44.5%	48.1%	3.6%
SAN FRANCISCO	215,953	44.1%	46.1%	2.0%
SAN JOAQUIN	66,735	39.4%	42.7%	3.3%
SAN LUIS OBISPO	45,966	49.0%	52.9%	4.0%
SAN MATEO	135,123	38.8%	41.0%	2.2%
SANTA BARBARA*	67,627	49.4%	52.8%	3.4%
SANTA CLARA	275,673	39.1%	42.1%	3.1%
SANTA CRUZ *	72,460	55.6%	59.3%	3.7%

Sanders	Votes	Election Day	July 7	Gain
*7/5 update				
SHASTA	16,835	51.1%	53.6%	2.5%
SIERRA	521	56.4%	57.0%	0.7%
SISKIYOU	6,360	59.2%	61.2%	2.0%
SOLANO	61,353	42.7%	44.2%	1.5%
SONOMA	87,638	48.7%	48.7%	0.0%
STANISLAUS	46,743	44.1%	47.9%	3.8%
SUTTER *	7,486	44.4%	46.3%	1.8%
TEHAMA	5,027	50.9%	52.8%	1.9%
TRINITY	1,883	62.0%	64.3%	2.3%
TULARE *	24,306	40.7%	44.6%	3.8%
TUOLUMNE	7,025	47.9%	51.1%	3.2%
VENTURA	117,366	45.7%	48.4%	2.7%
YOLO	36,416	47.9%	51.5%	3.7%
YUBA	5,159	52.4%	53.7%	1.3%

	Period	Total	Sanders	Clinton	Margin
Election Day	June 7	3,442,623	1,502,043	1,940,580	-438,537
			43.63%	56.37%	-12.74%
Total Vote	June7-July7	5,097,033	2,373,218	2,723,815	-350,597
			46.56%	53.44%	-6.88%
Post Elect Day	June8-July7	1,654,410	871,175	783,235	87,940
			52.66%	47.34%	5.32%

Covert Shredding of Provisional Ballots

A San Diego County Registrar insider claims that hundreds of thousands of California Democratic primary provisional ballots <u>were illegally destroyed</u> in a covert shredding operation.

A consignment of boxes was delivered to the San Diego Registrar's Office at 5600 Overland Ave in the morning and an "oversized shredding van" arrived minutes later and took the boxes away. The boxes were carried from the building to the vehicle by men she had never seen before wearing dark blue overalls.

CA Vote Timeline (does not include nearly 1,000,000 NPP ballots)

		Votes	HRC	Sanders	HRC	Sanders
Election Day	June 7 early	1,520,626	951,304	557,005	62.56%	36.63%
	June 7 late	1,949,824	977,447	945,080	50.13%	48.47%
Election Day	**Total**	**3,470,450**	**1,928,750**	**1,502,085**	**55.58%**	**43.28%**
June 8-23	Vote by Mail	1,313,293	645,090	652,707	49.12%	49.70%
June 7-23	**Total**	**4,783,743**	**2,573,840**	**2,154,792**	**53.80%**	**45.04%**
June7 late to final		3,263,117	1,622,536	1,597,786	**49.72%**	**48.97%**
June 9-23	Provisional	301,824	120,247	179,163	39.84%	59.36%
	Est. Provisionals	100,000	33,280	66,000	33.28%	66.00%
	NPP	995,000	288,550	706,450	29.00%	71.00%
	Total	**1,396,824**	**442,077**	**951,613**	**31.65%**	**68.13%**
	Total	**6,180,567**	**3,015,917**	**3,106,404**	**48.80%**	**50.26%**
			90,488			**1.46%**
	Total-June7 early	**4,659,941**	**2,064,613**	**2,549,399**	**44.31%**	**54.71%**

Update

Brakey total Estimated	**6,180,567**	
6/7 Elect Day Counted	3,470,450	
Uncounted	2,710,117	
7/7 Unctd Counted	2,353,152	
Remain Unctd	356,965	
Missing	686,210	
7/7 Unctd+missing	**1,043,175**	
75% Sanders	782,381	Uncounted + missing
25% Clinton	260,794	Uncounted + missing
Sanders gain	**521,588**	
Clinton margin	426,665	on June 7
Bernie margin	**94,922**	on July 7
Greg Palast Estimated	**100,000**	

CA Ballot Count Timeline

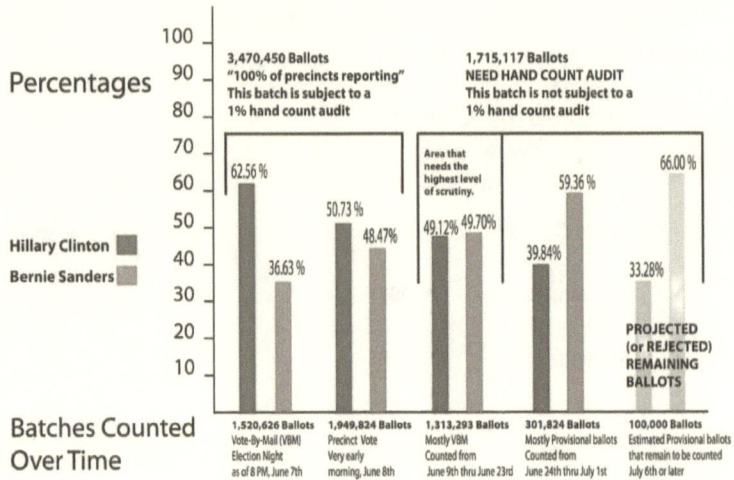

Vote Share Sensitivity Analysis

CASE I	2014 Party ID	Sanders	Clinton
Dem	43.0%	45.0%	55.0%
Ind	29.0%	65.0%	35.0%
Total	72.0%	38.2%	33.8%
	2-party	53.1%	46.9%
Sanders % Ind			
%Dem	60.0%	65.0%	70.0%
50.0%	54.0%	56.0%	58.1%
45.0%	51.0%	53.1%	55.1%
40.0%	48.1%	50.1%	52.1%

CASE II	2016 Party ID	Sanders	Clinton
Dem	30.0%	45.0%	55.0%
Ind	45.0%	65.0%	35.0%
Total	75.0%	42.8%	32.3%
	2-party	57.0%	43.0%
Sanders % Ind			
%Dem	60.0%	65.0%	70.0%
50.0%	56.0%	59.0%	62.0%
45.0%	54.0%	57.0%	60.0%
40.0%	52.0%	55.0%	58.0%

CASE III	2014 Party ID	Sanders	Clinton
Dem	43.0%	35.0%	65.0%
Ind	29.0%	60.0%	40.0%
Total	72.0%	32.5%	39.6%
	2-party	45.1%	54.9%

Sanders % Ind

%Dem	55.0%	60.0%	65.0%
40.0%	46.0%	48.1%	50.1%
35.0%	43.1%	45.1%	47.1%
30.0%	40.1%	42.1%	44.1%

CASE IV	2016 Party ID	Sanders	Clinton
Dem	30.0%	35.0%	65.0%
Ind	45.0%	60.0%	40.0%
Total	75.0%	37.5%	37.5%
	2-party	50.0%	50.0%

Sanders % Ind

%Dem	55.0%	60.0%	65.0%
40.0%	49.0%	52.0%	55.0%
35.0%	47.0%	50.0%	53.0%
30.0%	45.0%	48.0%	51.0%

5. Mainstream Media

Corporate media election analysts claim that there is no proof of election fraud and that exit polls are unreliable:

- Early/absentee voting favored Clinton
- Differential response: Sanders voters were more motivated
- Young Sanders voters were more likely to respond
- Uncounted ballots
- Vote audits
- Vulnerable voting machines

An analysis of **early/absentee** voting assumed the official results were correct, but that the exit polls were incorrect due to early/absentee voting. The early/absentee margins required were calculated to match the vote by making various estimates of the early/absentee vote in proportion to the total vote.

The margins made sense in Florida, North Carolina and Texas but not in Connecticut, Georgia, Ohio, Oklahoma and South Carolina. These states were inconclusive: Arkansas, Indiana, Maryland, Michigan and Tennessee

Did Sanders do better in the exit polls because his supporters were **enthusiastic** and more willing to talk to exit pollsters? In 2004, exit pollsters Mitofsky-Edison proposed the reluctant Bush responder theory (rBr) to explain why Kerry did so much better in the exit polls than in the vote. But it was disproven by data which compared response rates and Kerry support by precinct.

Sanders drew larger crowds and outraised Clinton. But a Gallup poll from late March showed Clinton supporters far more enthusiastic: 54% of Clinton supporters were extremely or very enthusiastic, compared to 44% of Sanders. Pre-election polls on Super Tuesday and March 8 gave Clinton an enthusiasm advantage in every state but Vermont. Clinton leads in enthusiasm yet the exit polls understate her support. Trump's big lead in enthusiasm has no effect on the exit poll discrepancies.

If an enthusiasm gap does affect exit poll response rates, Sanders' support in the exit polls should be significantly lower. The exact opposite is true.

Sanders led decisively among the **18-29 age group**. Edison Research tracks which age groups refuse to be polled and adjusts the weights accordingly. Ted Soares analyzed the correlation between the exit poll discrepancies and Sanders' performance among young voters. If oversampling the 18-29 vote is inflating Sanders' share in the exit polls, the effect should be magnified when Sanders does better among the young. In fact, the opposite happens:

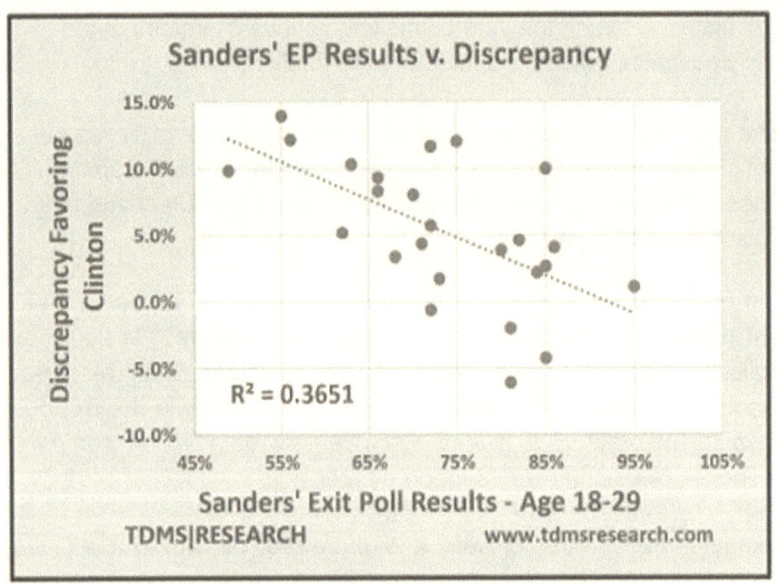

There's a slight negative correlation: the exit polls match more closely when more young voters support Sanders. But if age is the best predictor of candidate support, Sander's performance is meaningful. If his support is low among the young, it's even lower with older demographics.

Soares' graph contradicts the logic of the youth oversampling theory. If younger voters are oversampled, it should help Sanders. The discrepancy should increase if he has higher support among those voters. The exact opposite occurred. The youth oversampling theory fails state-by-state and overall.

Since the most common polling error theories can't explain the recurring discrepancies favoring Clinton, it indicates that the exit polls aren't the problem. If the discrepancies can't be explained by random error *or* systematic bias, then it's likely the exit polls are accurate and it's logical to believe that the exit polls successfully captured voter intent.

Did the Democratic primary exit polls include voters whose ballots weren't **counted?** If the ballots were mostly for Bernie Sanders, it could explain why the exit polls consistently had him doing better. In the 2000 election, there were more than 5 million uncounted ballots (180,000 were spoiled in Florida). Approximately 3.5 million (70%) were Al Gore votes. Therefore Gore won by at least 2 million more votes than his recorded 540,000 margin.

In the primaries, hundreds of thousands were forced to vote on provisional ballots. If a voter is denied at the polls (i.e., registration confusion, voter ID, etc.), they can cast a provisional ballot which is supposed to be reviewed later. Provisional ballots are a potential problem in exit polling. Edison does not ask voters if they voted provisionally. If voters used provisional ballots, were exit polled and had their ballots rejected, the exit polls could be skewed.

In the primaries before May, over 220,000 provisional ballots were uncounted. About half were from New York and Arizona: 91,000 from New York City alone, and 20,000 more from Maricopa County.

Maricopa County officials suggested that large numbers of independents erroneously tried to vote in the primary. Arizona's Democratic primary is closed; only registered Democrats can participate. If independents tried to vote provisionally, their ballot would be rejected. Apart from Yavapai County, Arizona had no exit polling.

New York was polled and was a closed primary. Large numbers of independents voting provisionally could partially explain New York's 12% discrepancy? Independents heavily favored Bernie Sanders.

There are numerous accounts of voters in closed primary states (Arizona, New York, and others) having their registration mysteriously changed. Most were registered Democrats who had their party affiliation switched or were purged from the rolls. Either one would have barred them from the closed primaries, leaving them no choice but to vote provisionally.

Since polling error can't explain the Clinton shift, the exit polls reflected voter intent. And the failure of the uncounted ballots explanation leaves no legitimate reason for the official results not to. We're left only with an illegitimate reason - vote rigging in favor of Hillary Clinton.

Many suspected vote rigging in Clinton's favor from the beginning. But there wasn't any proof until April, when fraudulent vote counts in Chicago were revealed. Illinois mandates a 5% **hand-count audit** to verify the machines' accuracy. Paper audit trails from the DRE machines are tallied by hand and compared against the machine counts. Multiple citizen observers who watched Chicago's audit gave disturbing testimony:

The auditors tried to hide the count from observers, clearly not wanting to be overseen. Multiple times, the hand count differed from the machine count, so the auditors changed their hand tally to match. In one precinct, 21 Sanders votes were erased and 49 Clinton votes were added, in order to match the machine count. Several observers came forth with matching testimony and affidavits.

Chicago's audit provided the first concrete evidence that machines were miscounting votes. Miscounts occurred in many precincts, with the machines nearly always favoring Clinton. The fact that one candidate consistently benefits makes it unlikely that it was random occurrence. Voting machines in Chicago were definitely rigged in Clinton's favor - and it probably happened elsewhere.

If exit poll discrepancies indicate vote rigging, greater discrepancies should have occurred where the machines are more vulnerable. Analysis of voting systems and audit procedures in each state is a confirmation.

Large exit polling discrepancies match up with the vote rigging pattern. The only states that don't are New Hampshire (4.2% discrepancy for Sanders), Massachusetts (8.0% for Clinton), Texas (9.3% for Clinton), and Maryland (0.6% for Sanders). Massachusetts fits the pattern when only college towns are analyzed, implying that college towns in particular were targeted. The other three states deserve further analysis. Overall, though, the correlation is quite strong, reinforcing the idea that the exit poll discrepancies indicate vote rigging.

http://www.counterpunch.org/2016/05/11/hillary-clinton-versus-bernie-sanders-in-depth-report-on-exit-polling-and-election-fraud-allegations/

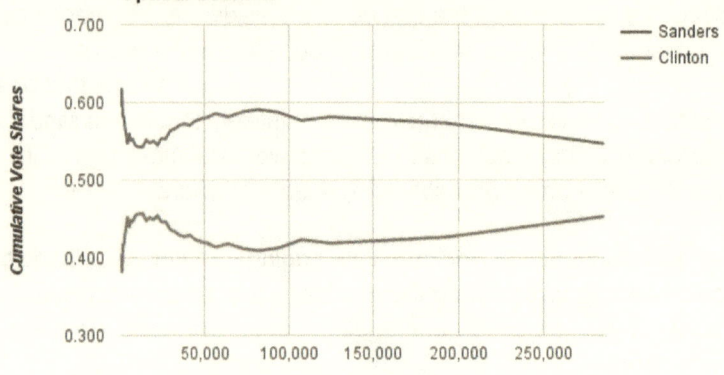

MI Primary Cumulative Vote Shares: AccuVote Optical Scanner

Cumulative Votes - smallest to largest counties

Rebutting Mainstream Media Propaganda

The mainstream media always attempts to dismiss the overwhelming evidence of exit polls as indicators of election fraud.

Actor and dedicated progressive activist Tim Robbins tweeted on the exit poll discrepancies. Joshua Holland wrote an article in The Nation criticizing Robbins, Lee Camp, Bob Fitrakis, Professor Steven Freeman and myself.

Our responses are included. Although the responses may appear to be redundant, they are in fact unique arguments and perspectives which collectively put to rest the naysayer propaganda.

Nate Cohn wrote a NY Times article declaring that the 2000 and 2004 presidential elections and 2016 Democratic primaries were not stolen.

Nate Silver wrote an article giving ten reasons why exit polls should be ignored. Nate never mentioned the fraud factor as a possible cause of the exit poll discrepancies.

Joseph Lenski of Edison Research posted on exit poll methodology but never mentioned the fraud factor.

Joshua Holland in the Nation Magazine

On Tim Robbins, election fraud and how nonsense spreads around the Internet.

Monday, actor Tim Robbins caused a stir when he tweeted out a Facebook meme, charging that CNN and The New York Times are blind to a massive conspiracy going on right beneath their noses. It had close to 1,000 retweets when Robbins apparently deleted it. A quick glance is enough to know that there are problems with the meme. The exit poll numbers are wrong.

In Massachusetts, for example, CNN reported that exit polls showed Clinton winning by 2 points, which is very close to her 1.4 percent margin in the final results. In Alabama, CNN reports the exit polls showing Clinton with a 57-point margin, the Facebook meme claims it was 44.7 points, and the final result was 60.4 percent. But where did Tim Robbins come up with these numbers? I decided to do a bit of reporting, and I ended up chasing this Facebook meme down a rabbit-hole of misinformation and conspiracism. It offers a pretty good case-study of how bullshit can come to dominate our online discourse.

The meme was created by Lee Camp, a political comedian who hosts a weekly show on RT, the Russian foreign news network. It has over 2,000 shares on Facebook as of this writing. Via email, I asked Camp for his source, and he pointed me to a post on Reddit by a user who goes by the handle "turn-trout." Turn-trout, who didn't respond to a message seeking comment, claims that these are unadjusted exit polls, and links to a spreadsheet purportedly showing wide discrepancies between the raw data and the final results.

The spreadsheet was created by Richard Charnin, who writes a blog devoted to "JFK conspiracy and systemic election fraud analysis." Charnin's spreadsheet appears to be the basis of a broad swath of viral Internet content alleging widespread election theft during the 2016 primaries, including the work of Free Press editors Harvey

Wasserman and Bob Fitrakis. *Charnin seems to think that exit polls can reveal that virtually all our elections have been rigged, writing, "in the 1988-2008 presidential elections, the Democrats won the exit polls by 52-42%; they won the recorded vote by just 48-46%, an 8% discrepancy."*

Virtually all of these claims are based on the idea that exit polls are a telltale sign of fraud. In a follow-up tweet, Tim Robbins _explained_ that, "exit polls are historically pretty accurate," and "are a heads-up on vote tampering." Turn-trout agrees, writing, "Exit polls have historically and throughout the world been used as a check against, and rough indicator of, the degree of election fraud."

This is also the basis of claims by Wasserman and Fitrakis – who point to _the precision of German exit polling_ to emphasize the point – and Steven Freeman, a Penn State psychologist who authored the book, _Was the 2004 Presidential Election Stolen?: Exit Polls, Election Fraud, and the Official Count_.

So there you have it. They say a lie can travel halfway around the world before the truth can get its boots on, and that's especially true of the internet. Here we have an example of an actor citing a comedian who picked up a claim from an an anonymous Reddit user citing preliminary exit poll data put together by a JFK conspiracy theorist. Bringing it all full circle is The Hill, which ran a story titled, "_Actor Tim Robbins blames Sanders losses on 'voter fraud,_'" which will no doubt be shared thousands of times on Facebook and Twitter.

If Hillary Clinton entered the race with a very large lead in the national polls and an enormous amount of support from Democratic Party activists and elected officials, as she did, and then quickly built up a significant lead in pledged delegates, as she did, then at no time since the start of the race, regardless of how unscrupulous her campaign might be, would there be any rational motive for risking infamy by rigging the vote. You don't need to cheat when you're winning.

That didn't sit well with Harvey Wasserman and Bob Fitrakis, whose earlier piece for The Free Press, "Is the 2016 election already being stripped & flipped?," I had mentioned briefly in the column. They've now published a lengthy broadside accusing me, and The Nation, of not being able to handle the truth when it comes to "election theft." (It's an odd charge, given that my Nation colleague Ari Berman has done some of the best reporting in the country on vote suppression.).

It's unfortunate that Wasserman and Fitrakis didn't engage my argument (or link to my piece so that readers might judge it for themselves). Instead, they waved away the idea that looking at motive is a legitimate way of evaluating the likelihood that a crime has been committed, writing that the argument was "a bit hard to follow."

My Response to Josh Holland

Holland called the analysis of exit polls it a "rabbit hole of misinformation and conspiracism". I have concluded based on 15 years of posting that when a naysayer uses the conspiracy meme, he will invariably proceed with misinformation and factual omission. Holland was no exception.

Holland did not mention my two advanced degrees in applied mathematics or that I have followed presidential elections since 1952. He referred to me as a JFK Conspiracy Theorist, as if that disqualifies me from analyzing election fraud. That was a big mistake; he apparently believes in the thoroughly debunked Single Bullet Theory. That tells me all I need to know. As is typical of naysayers and corporate media shills, Holland failed to do his homework on the statistically impossible number of exit poll discrepancies proving election fraud and the statistically impossible number of unnatural JFK witness deaths proving a conspiracy.

He only succeeded in exposing himself as an incompetent researcher. Holland said that the exit poll results are "wrong". How does he know that? Where is his supporting data and analysis? He has obviously not viewed the nearly pristine unadjusted data downloaded from CNN, yet he calls the numbers "bullshit". That says it all. His articles are biased and misleading; they will not fool those who are aware of the facts and the math that proves election fraud.

Holland interviewed Joe Lenski of Edison Research. But he failed to get Lenski to explain why exit pollsters force a match to the recorded vote – even if the recorded vote is bogus. Lenski does not logically explain why ALL exit polls are matched to the recorded vote counts. He has never provided a rationale for the match.

Lenski works for the Corporate Media (the National Election Pool) – just like Holland, who apparently fails to see the significance. He never considers that the recorded vote may be fraudulent. In fact, he never mentions the F-word – nor does anyone else in the corporate media. Holland fails to see the significance of that. Holland wrote that Lenski stressed that "*pre-election polls are also adjusted to conform their samples to what pollsters know about the populations they're trying to measure. The irony of all of this is that the adjusted data are far more accurate than the raw data*". If that is the case why won't the pollsters show us the raw exit poll data in the precincts"?

Are we supposed to take that comment seriously?
Apparently Holland does. If that is the case why won't the pollsters show us the raw exit poll data in all the precincts polled? And how did they end up with an exact 0.01% match to the recorded vote in the CT primary?

In spreadsheets linked from my blog, I provide 1988-2008 historical presidential vote and unadjusted exit poll data. The Democrats led the exit polls by 52-42% but led the recorded vote by just 48-46%. The probability of the 8% discrepancy is one in trillions. Holland does not have a clue about Probability and Statistics 101. He does not appreciate or comprehend the magnitude of the discrepancy. The data is available if he would care to truly investigate.

The data shows that 135 of 274 state presidential exit polls from 1988-2008 exceeded the margin of error - and 131 moved in a "redshift" to the GOP. The probability is ZERO: E-116. That's 116 zeros after the decimal. Holland does not appreciate or comprehend the magnitude of the discrepancy.

Sanders has won 12 of 13 caucuses, but only 6 of 27 primaries. Election fraud anomalies were apparent in NY MA IL AZ IA NV OH DE WY WI MO DE MI AL TN GA AR TX.

Sanders led hand-counted precincts in Massachusetts by 17%, while machine counted precincts went to Clinton by 2%.

The CNN NY Primary exit poll indicated that Sanders had 48% (officially he had 42.1%). But he may have done better than 48% since ALL exit polls are adjusted throughout the day to the recorded vote. And hundreds of thousands of voters were disenfranchised when their registrations were flipped or dropped altogether.

There was an 11.8% discrepancy between the NY exit poll (52-48%) and the recorded vote (57.9-42.1%). The probability of the discrepancy is 1 in 120,000.

Sanders exit poll share declined from the poll to the vote in 21 of 23 primaries. The probability P = 1 in 30,000 = BINOMDIST (2, 23, 0.5, true).

Sanders exit poll share exceeded his recorded share by more than the margin of error in 9 of the 23 primaries. The probability of this result being due to chance: P= 1 in 441 million = 1- BINOMDIST (8, 23, 0.025, false).

As usual, in the recent CT, MD and PA primaries, the exit poll was forced to match the recorded vote. The differences between Clinton's

2-party adjusted exit poll share and the recorded share were: CT
.01%; MD 0.10%; PA -.17%.

The mainstream media (including *The Nation*) won't dare touch the
Third Rail - ELECTION FRAUD. They never discuss malicious,
proprietary voting machines and central tabulators that were built to
flip the votes. Will Holland look at the evidence which proves that the
primaries are being stolen from Sanders and write about it?

Tim Robbins' response to Holland

We Need to Fix Our Election System

*Going into Tuesday's Democratic primary in Indiana, polls showed
Bernie Sanders trailing Hillary Clinton by around 7 percent. The final
tally had Sanders up by 6 percent, a 13 point difference that seems
to follow a pattern of polling discrepancies in this primary process
that are quite troubling. A couple of weeks ago I shared a post
containing statistics compiled from CNN and the New York Times
figures comparing Democratic Party primary exit polls and final
election results. The numbers show a significant discrepancy
between the two, favoring Hillary Clinton in all but one of the
primaries by an average of 9.02 percent and in the New York primary
by 16 percent. The post carried an incendiary headline, suggesting
election fraud, which caused quite a ruckus. I'm glad it did. We need
to have this discussion.*

*This posting led to the predictable onslaught of internet trolls calling
me crazy, conspiracy theorist, etc., all the talking points that are
being masterminded by the sleaze-meisters over at David Brock's
Correct the Record, a Hillary Clinton Super PAC. The post also
brought criticism from the mainstream media, but that is no surprise
to me. I've been there before. In the 2002-3 campaign to stop the
Iraq war, others and I were characterized as crazy, conspiracy
theorists, etc., as mainstream media shamefully abdicated its role in
a functioning democracy by becoming a propaganda arm for Bush*

and Co. Yes. The New York Times did that, and the Washington Post and ABC, CBS, NBC, CNN, MSNBC, FOX News, PBS, NPR etc.

We, the millions who across the world were saying no, who were aware of the lies that Bush and Co. were telling, were ignored by the mainstream media, marginalized as radicals and told by pundits to shut our unpatriotic mouths. So when that happened to me again two weeks ago, often by the same organizations that had marginalized me for my opposition to the war in 2002-3, I recognized the familiarity of it all. Could my post have touched a nerve? It certainly did with Joshua Holland, who wrote in Raw Story that I was involved with a "rabbit hole of misinformation and conspiracism." He then goes on to refute the claims of election fraud with seemingly empirical statistical evidence. Now, I am not a mathematician. But Richard Charnin is. He took issue with Mr. Holland's article. I defer to his expertise: "Election Fraud: Response to Joshua Holland."

Professor Bob Fitrakis Social Science Statistics 101

Dear Mr. Holland: After studying and assessing your work this semester, it is with deep regret that I have to inform you that you failed Social Science Statistics 101.

As you know, you have characterized us as "conspiracy theorists" because in our STRIP & FLIP SELECTION OF 2016: FIVE JIM CROWS & ELECTRONIC ELECTION THEFT, Harvey Wasserman and I have suggested that exit polls matter. You have also publicly denounced our colleague Richard Charnin, who has two separate Master's degrees in Applied Mathematics, for his analysis of this year's primary exit poll results versus election results.

Since you show so little interest in statistical analysis, let me briefly go over what you should know: First of all, exit polls are the accepted international standard for indications of election fraud and vote tampering. Here I refer you to Eric Bjornlund and Glenn Cowan's 2011 pamphlet Vote Count Verification: a User's Guide for Funders,

Implementers and Stakeholders. *Their work, done under the auspices of Democracy International for the US Agency for International Development (USAID), outlines how exit polling is used to ensure free and fair elections.*

When election results do not match exit poll results, we should not simply accept these results. What Charnin does, and has been doing for many years, is studying improbable election results that fall statistically outside the "margin of error" (MoE).

For example, Ohio primary exit polls indicated that Clinton would win 51.4% to Sanders' 47.6%. She was expected to win by 3.8%. The actual vote indicated she won 56.5% to 43%. Clinton won the election by 13.8% which was 10 percentage points more than the exit polls indicated.

Statistics tell us that the correct Ohio MoE was 3.12% based on N=1670 respondents. There is a 0.1% probability that the 5.1% exit poll discrepancy from the recorded vote was due to chance. Therefore there is a 99.9% probability that the official Ohio primary results were improbable.

These results should trigger further investigative analysis. Take a look at Charnin's statistics at this post for Democratic primary MoE and probability calculations
https://richardcharnin.wordpress.com/catogory/2016-election/

Beth Clarkson response to Holland
http://showmethevotes.org/2016/06/10/the-theater-is-on-fire/

Sadly, Mr. Holland does not understand the math well enough to realize that, despite the protests of the professional pollster interviewed, claims of widespread fraud are not baseless. Exit poll results for the democratic presidential primary provide not one but two solid pieces of evidence in the case for widespread election fraud.

We have a voting system, as he acknowledges, that gives us no cause for confidence that our voting results are accurately assessed. Despite this, he claims that there is no cause for concern. I disagree as I find multiple independent paths of analyses give evidence that consistently points to massive widespread election fraud across our country.

My specialty is statistics and I've pulled down publicly available data independently, analyzed it myself, and corroborated analyses which points to massive widespread election fraud. Mr. Holland disparages the mathematical work of Richard Charnin. He disparages him for writing about the murder of JFK. Is it really foolish to think that someone besides Lee Harvey Oswald was involved? I have not found an error in any of the analyses of his that I have repeated. In particular, his assessment of the binomial probability regarding the likelihood of the exit poll results, is both accurate and appropriate. I have verified it myself. This binomial analysis was ignored by Mr. Holland in favor of criticizing a different approach that was also used. That approach is also sound, but I have not reproduced those calculations. That both models show results that are consistent with the hypothesis of election fraud is more than doubly damning.

The excuses Mr. □ Lenski, Edison's executive vice president is quoted as providing are specious with regard to the magnitude of the anomalies we are seeing. Yes, there are issues that can lead to inherent problems due the different ways they performed the surveys. No, those reasons are not sufficient to explain the anomalies we are seeing across the country. There are only two possibilities – a) Bernie supporters are more likely to respond to the poll or b) there is widespread election fraud altering election results in favor of Hillary across the U.S.

While we can never completely eliminate (a), Mr. Lenski's excuse is no more than a restatement of that first hypothesis while he notes that there is a lower response rate (how much lower?) for the more detailed surveys conducted in the U.S. While it's easy for the mathematically naive to infer causality from his statement, that isn't automatically the case. Further, it's not an assumption that should be made without explicitly stating it. It's also a testable assumption, but Mr. Lenski's firm is the only entity with access to the data to do the test.

So which do you think is more likely across the U.S.: Are Bernie voters just more civic-minded and willing to participate in exit polls than Hillary voters or is some well-organized group of wealthy individuals able to successfully conspire to fix voting machines across the nation or are multiple independent local political actors across the country taking advantage of the non-transparent hackable voting systems? While you contemplate those options and estimate the probability of the first hypothesis with respect to the last two, let me review some of the additional evidence in support of the hypothesis of fraud. Cumulative Vote Share (CVS) analysis pioneered by Francis Choquette shows problems across the nation for the past decade or more. Interestingly enough, places that use hand counted ballots do not show the same trends and within a state, analyzing by machine can show sharply different trends for different equipment. Such analysis shows trends that are indicative of rigging that favors Hillary

The apparent ease of hacking electronic voting machines combined with the prevalence of election rigging through-out the world and human history. Lack of basic quality control procedures: In most locations in the U.S., no one – not officials and not citizens – actually verify the official vote counts. Canvassing becomes a sham that involves verifying that yes, the machine produced outcomes all add up to the machine produced totals. In those places where the count was supposed to be publicly verified, citizens watching report blatant miscounting to force a match to the "official results". Their testimony to election commissioners about such actions were met with a blank stare followed by dismissal of their testimony.

A few questions for Mr. Holland: Did you spontaneously decide to write about this? A reaction to a disparaging blog regarding a previous piece saying "don't worry, the theater is NOT on fire" vis-a-vis election fraud. Or was it suggested? Assigned? Did your publisher encourage you to disparage these claims, despite your lack of expertise to regarding either surveys or statistics. Would a favorable opinion piece regarding such claims have been published?

*Mr Holland, you have not done the analysis for yourself. You base your opinion of its significance on the expert opinion you trust – Mr. Lenski, an executive of the polling company. My response is that I have looked into this deeply and I trust my own expert opinion on this matter. It is a justifiable conclusion that widespread election fraud is going on in this country. **The Theater is on fire.** We need to take care of this problem now! The fix, btw, is both easy and impossible. All we have to do is demand a transparent and accurate vote count from our election officials.*

My Response to Nate Cohn

In his recent New York Times article, Nate Cohn reverts to classic exit poll naysayer talking points that have been debunked long ago. I thought I was done debunking their posts.

Ever since the 2000 election, exit poll naysayers have stated a) Edison Research claims that their exit polls aren't designed to detect fraud; b) the sample size is too small and c) the questions are too lengthy and complex.

Sample size? Big enough so that the MoE was exceeded in 11 of 26 Democratic primary exit polls – a 1 in 77 billion probability. Questions too lengthy? You mean asking males and females who they voted for? Not designed to detect fraud? That is true; unadjusted exit polls are adjusted to match the corrupt recorded vote – and cover up the fraud.

Nate must be unaware of this fact: According to a recent Harvard study, the US ranks last (#47) in election integrity.

http://thefreethoughtproject.com/land-free-ranks-dead-west-fair-elections/ .

According to Nate, the exit polls are always wrong. He maintains that they were wrong in the 2000 and 2004 elections and that Bush won both elections fairly; there was no fraud. It is common knowledge that Bush stole both elections. This is proven by the mathematically impossible exit poll discrepancies, True Vote Model and Cumulative Vote Share analysis. Unadjusted exit polls were close to the True Vote. The discrepancies were due to corrupted vote counts, not bad polling.

Historical evidence of fraud is based on a recurring pattern: The vast majority of exit polls that exceed the margin of error favor the progressive candidate. Virtually all exit polls shift to the establishment candidate in the recorded vote. Nate ignores or is ignorant of the overwhelming evidence proving that the Democratic primary was stolen. He cannot refute these facts:

– Sanders' exit poll share exceeded his recorded share in 24 of the 26 primaries exit polled. The probability is 1 in 190,000.

– Sanders exit poll share exceed his recorded share by more than the margin of error in 11 of the 26 primaries. The probability is 1 in 77 billion.

Is the exit poll shift to Clinton just pure luck? Or is something else going on? Let's review and debunk Nate's comments.

NC *I didn't write about this during the primary season, since I didn't want to dignify the views of conspiracy theorists. But they're still going. The exit polls are a sufficient basis to make this determination, in the eyes of the conspiracists, because exit polls are used internationally to detect fraud. They're supposedly very accurate.*

RC Note the immediate use of the term conspiracy theorist; a sure sign of an Internet troll. But Nate is not a troll; he's writing for the NY Times.

NC *All of this starts with a basic misconception: that the exit polls are usually pretty good. I have no idea where this idea comes from, because everyone who knows anything about early exit polls knows that they're not great. The 2000, 2004, 2008 exit polls were biased. Kerry and Gore both lost.*

In 2004, the exit polls showed John Kerry easily winning an election he clearly lost — with both a huge error and systematic bias outside of the "margin of error." *The national exits showed Kerry ahead by three points (and keep in mind the sample size on the national exit is vastly larger than for a state primary exit poll) and leading in states like Virginia, Ohio and Florida — which all went to George W. Bush.*

The story was similar in 2000. The early exit polls showed Al Gore winning Alabama, Arizona, Colorado and North Carolina. Mr. Bush won these states by 6-15 points. In 2008 the exit polls showed a pretty similar bias toward Barack Obama. The same thing happened in 1996. It was actually even worse in 1992. The exit polls had Bill Clinton winning Texas, which went to George H.W. Bush, and basically everywhere.

RC Kerry clearly won. It wasn't even close.

2004: Overwhelming Statistical Proof of a Stolen Election

2004: Simple Arithmetic Proof that Bush Stole the election

To believe Bush won in 2004 you must believe...

Al Gore won easily. It wasn't even close. 2000: Unadjusted Exit Polls indicate Gore won by 51-45% (5-7 million votes)

In 2008, Obama's landslide was denied by massive fraud.
2008: To believe Obama won by just 9.5 million-votes,,,
Proof that Obama won by much more than 9.5 million votes
2008 Unadjusted Exit Polls Confirm the True Vote Model

Clinton won in 1992 and 1996 by far greater margins than recorded.
https://docs.google.com/spreadsheets/d/1EWaKPDUolqbN7_od8sS
TNMRObfUidlVPRBxeyyirbLM/edit#gid=15

NC *The allegations are remarkably consistent. They go like this: Mr. Sanders did better in the early exit polls than he did in the final result. Therefore, Mrs. Clinton probably stole the election. The exit polls are a sufficient basis to make this determination, in the eyes of the conspiracists, because exit polls are used internationally to detect fraud. They're supposedly very accurate and "well controlled" (where this phrase comes from, I don't know). Sources for exit poll error — even more than in an ordinary poll: Differential non-response, Cluster effects, Absentee voters aren't included. Exit polls can be very inaccurate and systematically biased.*

RC The differential response canard was disproved in 2004 by the exit pollsters own data. The pollsters estimate absentee voters in their projections. Exit polls vary in accuracy, but the weighted average of a group of state polls in a given election will approximate the true vote. When an exit poll exceeds the margin of error, there is a 97% probability of vote miscounting. In 274 presidential elections from 1988 to 2008, 135 exit polls exceeded the margin of error – 131 in favor of the Republican. In the 26 Democratic primaries in 2016, the margin of error was exceeded in 11. The probability is one in trillions.

Reluctant Bush Responder; Evaluation of Edison Mitofsky Election System 2004

Nate claims he has no idea where the "misconception" that exit polls are accurate comes from. They come from the experts cited below – not from the controlled MSM. He calls these experts "conspiracy theorists"; his misconception is assuming there is no such thing as Election Fraud.

Nate states that the sources of exit poll errors are greater than in "ordinary" polls. His claim that exit poll non-response, cluster effect and absentee voters are not considered is false; these factors are used in weighting the sample. An exit poll cluster effect (typically 30%) is added to the theoretical margin of error. And of course, in an exit poll unlike pre-election polls, voters are asked who they just voted for.

What about sources and methods of election fraud? What is the motivation of the MSM in forcing the unadjusted exit polls to match corrupted vote counts?

NC *Exit polls can be very inaccurate and systematically biased. With this kind of history, you can see why no one who studies the exit polls believes that they can be used as an indicator of fraud in the way the conspiracy theorists do.*

RC Nate expects rational viewers to believe that experts who study exit polls are conspiracy theorists because they have concluded that the polls are indicators of fraud. Does he truly believe these experts are delusional and/or incompetent in assuming that exit poll discrepancies (which exceed the margin of error) raise legitimate questions as to the likelihood of fraud?

Pollsters ask males and females in foreign countries the question "Who Did You Vote For" to check for possible election fraud. They ask the same question in the U.S. The difference is that here they essentially cover-up the fraud by adjusting the responses to match the recorded vote – and always assume ZERO fraud.

NC *Why are exit polls tilted toward Sanders? Young voters are far more likely to complete the polls. Voter registration files are just starting to be updated. Sanders is a candidate with historic strength among young voters.*

RC That is pure conjecture and not based on factual evidence. But this is not conjecture: more Sanders than Clinton voters (young and old) were disenfranchised. But Nate doesn't mention that fact? What about all of those independents and Democrats who never got to the polls because of voided registrations, long lines and closing of polling places?

NC *There are other challenges with exit polls in the primaries. Usually, the exit polls select precincts by partisanship — ensuring a good balance of Democratic and Republican precincts. This helps in a general election. It doesn't do as much good in a primary.*

RC Nate does not know how the precincts were selected. It's proprietary information. Why won't the exit pollsters tell us which precincts were polled? Since they don't, we must assume they have something to hide. The pollsters (actually the MSM) do not want analysts to compare precinct votes to the exit poll response. It's clear that they might find discrepancies which indicate a high probability of vote miscounts.

My Response to Nate Silver

In November 2008 Silver wrote Ten Reasons Why You Should Ignore Exit Polls. Earlier, I replied on his last-place ranking of pollster John Zogby .

The Signal is the 52-42% Democratic lead in the 1988-2008 unadjusted presidential state and national exit polls. The Noise is the media propaganda that the Democrats won by 48-46% as shown in the published adjusted polls. But we all know that it is standard operating procedure to force the exit polls to match the (bogus) recorded vote. The media wants the public to believe that Systemic Election Fraud is a myth.

Is Nate asking us to ignore a) the final adjusted exit polls which are ALWAYS forced to match the recorded vote or b) the unadjusted, preliminary state and national exit polls? If it's (a), then he must believe that election fraud is systemic since the pristine, unadjusted exit polls are always forced to match the recorded vote, even if it is fraudulent. If it's (b), then he must believe that election fraud is a myth and that the recorded vote reflects actual voter intent (i.e. the true vote). Based on his writings, it must be (b). After reading his "ten reasons", I came up with ten reasons why he never responded to my posts.

He wrote: "*Oh, let me count the ways. Almost all of this, by the way, is lifted from Mark Blumenthal's outstanding Exit Poll FAQ*". Mark was the original Mystery Pollster and has worked full-time since 2004 to debunk any references to exit polls as indicators of election fraud.

In June 2006, Robert F. Kennedy Jr. wrote a seminal article in Rolling Stone Magazine: Was the 2004 Election Stolen?. In a pitiful attempt to debunk RFK, Salon's Farhad Manjoo wrote Was the 2004 Election Stolen? No. Manjoo's hit piece contained factual errors and omissions and was fully debunked by a number of analysts. Mark Blumenthal defended Manjoo and smeared RFK in this piece: Is RFK, Jr. Right About Exit Polls?

I wrote <u>My Response to the Mystery Pollster's critique of RFK</u> and an <u>Open Letter to Mark Blumenthal of Pollster.com.</u> Now I will count the ways.

NS 1. *Exit polls have a much larger intrinsic margin for error than regular polls. This is because of what are known as cluster sampling techniques. Exit polls are not conducted at all precincts, but only at some fraction thereof. Although these precincts are selected at random and are supposed to be reflective of their states as a whole, this introduces another opportunity for error to occur (say, for instance, that a particular precinct has been canvassed especially heavily by one of the campaigns). This makes the margins for error somewhere between 50-90% higher than they would be for comparable telephone surveys.*

RC Exit polls have a much smaller margin of error than pre-election polls. It stands to reason that exit polls are more accurate than pre-election polls because a) those polled know exactly who they voted for and b) in pre-election polls, respondents might change their mind – or not vote.

Regarding cluster samples, exit pollsters Edison-Mitofsky state in the notes to the National Exit Poll as well as in the <u>NEP Methods Statement</u> that exit poll respondents were randomly-selected and the overall margin of error was 1%. Adding the standard 30% cluster effect raises the calculated 0.86% MoE to 1.1%.

I understand why Nate would claim that exit polls are inaccurate since he apparently believes that election fraud on voting machines is non-existent. He never discusses the fraud factor. So of course he would conclude that the exit poll discrepancies from the recorded vote indicate that the polls are wrong. His fundamental problem is that he fail to consider the possibility that the exit discrepancies from the recorded vote were the result of systematic election fraud. But that is typical of mainstream media pundits. If they discussed the fraud factor, they would be out of a job.

Nate claims that the final Likely Voter (LV) pre-election polls (which are a subset of all Registered Voters (RV) interviewed) are spot-on because they match the recorded vote. But LV polls always understate Democratic turnout, since the vast majority of voters who fail to pass the Likely Voter Cutoff Model are young, newly registered Democrats.

That's one reason why Democrats average higher in the RV polls than in LVs and the media avoids the RVs in the month prior to the election. Another factor is that telephone polls miss cell-phone users who are young and Democratic. Most important, pre-election polls have been shown to overweight Republicans based on prior bogus recorded votes.

NS 2. *Exit polls have consistently overstated the Democratic share of the vote. Many of you will recall this happening in 2004, when leaked exit polls suggested that John Kerry would have a much better day than he actually had. But this phenomenon was hardly unique to 2004. In 2000, for instance, exit polls had Al Gore winning states like Alabama and Georgia (!). If you go back and watch* The War Room, *you'll find George Stephanopolous and James Carville gloating over exit polls showing Bill Clinton winning states like Indiana and Texas, which of course he did not win.*

RC Once again, Nate assumes that the recorded vote was fraud-free. Of course the Democrats always do better in the exit polls than in the recorded vote. But did Nate ever consider why? It is a fact that millions of votes are uncounted in every election and the vast majority are Democratic (over 50% are in minority districts). The U.S. Census reported over 80 million net uncounted votes since 1968. You always assume that the recorded vote is the True Vote. Uncounted votes put the lie to that argument, not to mention votes switched at the DREs and central tabulators.

Nate claimed Clinton did not win Indiana or Texas. How does he know? Can he provide proof that the voting machines were not tampered with? In 1992 there were 9.4 million net uncounted votes, approximately 75% for Clinton. Clinton's margins were very plausible.

The exit polls indicated that Clinton won Indiana by 53-30% (Perot had 16%) and Texas by 43-32% (Perot had 25%). But they were both likely stolen by Bush. Clinton lost Indiana (42.9-36.8%) by 138,000 votes (330,000 uncounted). He lost Texas (40.6-37.1%) by 215,000 (663,000 uncounted). So had all the votes been counted, Clinton would have won both states. Note that we are not even considering vote-switching from Clinton or Perot to Bush, just the uncounted votes.

In 1996, there were 8.7 million net uncounted votes – again, approximately 75% for Clinton. Clinton won the Indiana exit poll by 50-40%, but Dole won the recorded vote by 117,000, 47.1-41.6% (230,000 net uncounted). The Texas exit poll was tied at 46-46%, but Dole won by 280,000 votes, 48.8-43.8% (700,000 net uncounted). Again, had all the votes been counted, Clinton would have likely won both. And this does not include vote switching from Clinton or Perot to Dole.

NS 3. *The polls were particularly bad in this year's (2008) primaries. They overstated Barack Obama's performance by an average of about 7 points.*

RC Rush Limbaugh's called for "Operation Chaos" in which he advised Republicans to cross over in the Democratic primaries and vote for Hillary Clinton. His objective was to deny Obama the nomination. Obama easily won the all the caucuses in which voters were visually counted.

NS 4. *Exit polls challenge the definition of a random sample. Although the exit polls have theoretically established procedures to collect a random sample — essentially, having the interviewer approach every nth person who leaves the polling place — in practice this is hard to execute at a busy polling place, particularly when the pollster may be standing many yards away from the polling place itself because of electioneering laws.*

RC Exit pollsters Edison-Mitofsky wrote in the notes to the 2004 National Exit Poll that respondents were randomly selected as they exited the polling booth.

NS 5. *Democrats may be more likely to participate in exit polls. Related to items #1 and #4 above, Scott Rasmussen has found that Democrats supporters are more likely to agree to participate in exit polls, probably because they are more enthusiastic about this election.*

RC Nate quotes a GOP pollster who never did an exit poll. There is no evidence that Democrats are more likely to participate. In fact, the historical data shows otherwise. Nate is resurrecting the reluctant Bush responder (rBr) hypothesis that was disproved by the exit pollster's own data in each of the 2000, 2004 and 2008 elections. It is also contradicted by a linear regression analysis which showed that response rates were highest in partisan GOP precincts and Red states. US Count Votes did a comprehensive analysis of the 2004 exit poll discrepancies which disproved the exit pollster's reluctant Bush responder hypothesis.

NS 6. *Exit polls may have problems calibrating results from early voting. Contrary to the conventional wisdom, exit polls will attempt account for people who voted before Election Day in most (although not all) states by means of a random telephone sample of such voters. However, this requires the polling firms to guess at the ratio of early voters to regular ones, and sometimes they do not guess correctly. In Florida in 2000, for instance, there was a significant underestimation of the absentee vote, which that year was a substantially Republican vote, leading to an overestimation of Al Gore's share of the vote, and contributing to the infamous miscall of the state.*

RC But Mitofsky claimed that the 2004 precinct design sample was near perfect. In the 2000 election, nearly 6 million ballots were never counted (a combination of spoiled, absentee and provisional) – and 75-80% were Gore votes – meaning that his True Vote margin was at least 3 million more than his recorded 540,000. And that is why Gore led the state exit poll aggregate by 50-45%.

Nate is either unaware or chooses to ignore the fact that in Florida there were over 180,000 spoiled ballots (113,000 double and triple-punched and 65,000 under-punched) that were never counted – and 75% were Gore votes. He apparently believe the myth that the spoiled ballots were due to stupid voters. He fails to mention the thousands of discarded Gore absentee ballots. GOP election officials discarded Democratic absentee ballots and included GOP ballots that were filed after the due date. And what about the Palm Beach butterfly ballot in which thousands of Jews were fooled into voting for Buchanan?

If Nate really believes that Bush won both the national and Florida elections in 2000, then he must also believe that a) the tooth fairy exists, b) global warming is just a hoax and c) the economic meltdown was due to natural supply and demand forces and that the economic forecasting models were at fault. He ignores the overwhelming evidence that the meltdown was due to corrupt global banksters gaming the financial system. Likewise, he ignores the election fraudsters that have systematically gamed the computers to miscount votes and prevent millions of eligible citizens from voting. To Nate it is all just noise, never human corruption.

NS 7. *Exit polls may also miss late voters. By "late" voters I mean persons who come to their polling place in the last couple of hours of the day, after the exit polls are out of the field. Although there is no clear consensus about which types of voters tend to vote later rather than earlier, this adds another way in which the sample may be nonrandom, particularly in precincts with long lines or extended voting hours.*

RC As a quant, Nate should ask how Kerry led by 51-48% at 12:22am (13047 respondents) but Bush led at 1:00am at the final (13660) after just 613 additional respondents? It's simple. The pollsters had to force the National to match the bogus recorded vote

(Bush 50.7-48.3%). It was impossible – a total sham. It was Kerry who led the final unadjusted NEP by 51.7-47.0%.

Exit polls are always forced to match the recorded vote. The 2004 adjusted final National Exit Poll indicated that 43% (52.6 million) of 2004 voters were returning Bush voters and 37% Gore voters. But Bush only had 50.5 million voters in 2000 – and approximately 2.5 million died. So there could not have been more than 48 million returning Bush voters. If 47 million turned out, there had to be 5.6 million phantom Bush voters. How does Nate explain that?

In 2008, Obama won the unadjusted National Exit Poll (17836 respondents) by 61-37%. But the poll was forced to match the recorded 52.9-45.6%. Obama had 52.4% of 121 million votes recorded on Election Day and 59.2% of the 10 million recorded later.

NS 8. *"Leaked" exit poll results may not be the genuine article. Sometimes, sources like Matt Drudge and Jim Geraghty have gotten their hands on the actual exit polls collected by the network pools. At other times, they may be reporting data from "first-wave" exit polls, which contain extremely small sample sizes and are not calibrated for their demographics. And at other places on the Internet (though likely not from Geraghty and Drudge, who actually have reasonably good track records), you may see numbers that are completely fabricated.*

RC The National Exit Poll timeline had Kerry leading by 51-48% at 4:00pm (8349 respondents), 9:00pm (11027) and 12:22am (13047). Kerry led at the final 13660 respondents by 51.7-47.0%. But at approximately 1:00am, Kerry responders were flipped to Bush in order to force the poll to match the recorded vote.

NS 9. *A high-turnout election may make demographic weighting difficult. Just as regular, telephone polls are having difficulty this cycle estimating turnout demographics — will younger voters and minorities show up in greater numbers? — the same challenges await exit pollsters. Remember, an exit poll is not a definitive record of what happened at the polling place; it is at best a random sampling.*

RC But high turnout is always good for the Democrats. That's why the GOP is always trying to suppress the vote. The National Exit Poll indicates that Kerry won 57-62% of new voters and that Obama had 72% of new voters in 2008. Nate now agrees that exit polls are indeed random samples and corrected point #4.

NS 10. *You'll know the actual results soon enough anyway. Have patience, my friends, and consider yourselves lucky: in France, it is illegal to conduct a poll of any kind within 48 hours of the election. But exit polls are really more trouble than they're worth, at least as a predictive tool. An independent panel created by CNN in the wake of the Florida disaster in 2000 recommended that the network completely ignore exit polls when calling particular states. I suggest that you do the same.*

RC Exit polls are more trouble than they are worth? Yes, that is true – for those who rig the elections. Exit polls were the first indicators that the 2004 election was stolen. Nate refuses to comprehend that Election Fraud is systemic – or that it even exists. He wants his readers to believe that the recorded vote accurately depicts true voter intent and the exit polls are always wrong.

In 2008, Obama had a recorded 52.9% share and won by 9.5 million votes. The unadjusted National Exit poll indicates that he won 61% of 17,836 respondents. He had 58.0% in the unadjusted state exit poll weighted aggregate (82,388 respondents) a 23 million vote margin - exactly matching the True Vote Model which used the same adjusted final NEP vote shares.

In 2004, Bush won the recorded vote by just 3 million but Kerry won the True Vote by 10 million. The Bush/Kerry 46/37% returning voter weights in the adjusted final 2008 NEP implied that there were 12 million more returning Bush than Kerry voters – an impossible 103% turnout of living Bush voters. Nate must agree that there could not have been 5 million returning third-party voters indicated by the final

2008 NEP since just 1.2 million were recorded in 2004. It's simple arithmetic.

The 1988-2008 unadjusted state and national presidential exit polls from the Roper site showed that the Democrats led the weighted average unadjusted polls by 52-42%, but by just 48-46% in the recorded vote.

The ultimate Smoking Gun: Of the 274 state exit polls listed on Roper for the 1988-2008 presidential elections, 135 exceeded the margin of error of which 131 "red-shifted" to the Republican and 4 to the Democrat. Only 14 would be expected to exceed the MoE at the 95% confidence level. The probability is E-116.

P=   0.0000000000   0000000000   0000000000   0000000000 0000000000 0000000000 0000000000 000000000 00000000000 0000000000 000000000 0000001.

My Response to Edison Research

Frustrated voters who have seen their elections stolen need to know the facts. The corporate media never discusses Election Fraud - the third-rail of American politics. But it is no longer the dirty little secret it was before the 2000 election.

The American Association for Public Opinion Research (AAPOR) discusses the matching process in Explaining Exit Polls. But they never mention election fraud as a likely cause of the discrepancies. Adjusted exit poll crosstabs contaminate the true statistical results as they do not reflect the actual responses of those polled.

In close races, the projection models also employ actual vote totals, first in sample precincts as it becomes available and then at the county level for all counties in a state as they become available.

It is important to note that after the votes have been counted, the exit poll results are adjusted to match the actual election outcomes. It is in this way that the final exit poll data can be used for its primary and most important purpose – to shed light on why the election turned out the way it did.

In the six presidential elections from 1988-2008, the Democrats won the unadjusted state and national exit polls by a 52-42%. The recorded margin was just 48-46%.

Edison Research conducts exit polls. In this report, ER once again fails to mention the Election Fraud factor, which has skewed the True Vote in national, state and local elections for decades.

http://statistical-research.com/wp-content/uploads/2014/08/Probability-Based-Exit-Poll-Estimation.pdf

ER *Of the surveys there were 19 states where the sample size was too small for individual state demographic or other breakouts.*

RC Unadjusted state exit poll data are a major component in calculating exit poll discrepancies. Having data for just 31 states made it impossible to compare the total weighted average of the state polls to the official recorded share. The decision was a blow to Election Integrity.

In 2012, the National Election Pool (NEP) of six media giants which funds the exit polls said it did not want to incur the cost, so they would not run exit polls in 19 states. That was a canard. Could it be that the NEP and the pollsters did not want the full set of 50 state exit polls to be used in a True Vote analysis? The continued pattern of discrepancies would just further reveal built-in systematic fraud. That is also why the question "How Did You Vote in 2008" was not published along with the usual cross tabs. The "How Voted" crosstab is the Smoking Gun of Election Fraud. In every election since 1988, the crosstab illustrates how pollsters adjust the number of returning Republican and Democratic voters (as well as the current vote shares) to match the recorded vote.

ER *The majority of interviews are conducted in-person on Election Day in a probability sample that is stratified based on geography and past vote.*

RC But the past recorded vote is biased for the Republicans. Any stratification strategy is therefore biased and favors the Republicans.

ER *The goal in this paper is not to provide a comprehensive and exhaustive discussion of the intricacies of the operational and statistical aspects of an exit poll but to provide additional discussion on various ways to incorporate probability distributions into an exit poll framework. The core of this discussion is based on discrete data in the exit poll. The examples used in this paper will be based on the data obtained from the 2012 presidential election and will specifically address the use of the Dirichlet and Normal distributions.*

RC There is nothing intricate about forcing unadjusted exit polls to match the recorded vote. It is quite simple. And it happens in every election. How does Edison explain the massive exit poll discrepancies?

In 2008, Obama had 61% in the National Exit Poll (17836 respondents) and 58% in the weighted aggregate of the state exit polls. But he had a 52.9% recorded share. The probability of the discrepancy is ZERO.

In 2004, John Kerry had 51.7% in the unadjusted National Exit Poll (13660 respondents)s. He led the state aggregate by 51.1-47.6%. But Kerry lost the recorded vote by 50.7-48.3%.

In 2000, Al Gore led the unadjusted National Exit Poll by 48.5-46.3%. He led the state aggregate polls by 50.8-44.4%. But Gore was held to a 48% tie with Bush in the recorded vote.

ER *A useful characteristic relating to probability distributions is the ability to use known data and then simulate from the posterior distribution. Using the exit poll framework, the statewide candidate estimates can be used and applied using the Dirichlet distribution approach. This means that the estimates from each state can be used to determine the probability that a given candidate will win each state. With the probability of success established for each state we can incorporate these probabilities into a winner-take-all Binomial distribution for all 50 states and the District of Columbia.*

RC A simulation is not required to calculate the expected electoral vote if we have calculated the state win probabilities, The expected EV is the product sum of the state win probabilities and corresponding electoral votes.
EV = SUMPRODUCT [prob(i) * EV(i)], where i =1,51.

In the 2012 True Vote Election Model, pre-election state win probabilities were calculated based on final Likely Voter (LV) polls. The model exactly projected Obama's 332 EV. But Obama's True Vote was much better than his recorded share. Note: LVs are a subset of Registered Voter (RV) polls which eliminate new, mostly Democratic, "unlikely" voters.

ER *Clearly, 'calling' a national election based purely on sample data is not the most favorable strategy due to sampling variability. However, updating the probability that a candidate will win with additional known data in each of the given states will decrease the variability in the posterior distribution. This can be accomplished by using additional known prior data or, as is often the case in elections, by adding the final precinct election results provided shortly after the polling places close.*

RC This assumes that the final precinct data has not been manipulated. In any case, a 10 million trial simulation is overkill. Only 500 Monte Carlo trials are necessary to calculate the probability of winning the electoral vote.

ER *This can be accomplished by using additional known prior data or, as is often the case in elections, by adding the final precinct election results provided shortly after the polling places close. Due to the nature of elections, informed priors are often available and can be incorporated into the estimates to improve the probability distribution. In this way, specific models can be developed to handle states with more or less available prior data and improve the overall model.*

We can take the currently collected data and model the results using other quantities that are available. In some ways, due to the nature of linear regression, prior information is already implicitly included in exit poll regression models.

RC *Again, no mention of votes being flipped in the precincts. But the prior election returning voter mix in five presidential elections was mathematically and physically impossible. The exit polls indicate that there were more returning Nixon and Bush voters from the prior election than were actually still alive. This is absolute proof that the published exit polls were adjusted to match vote-miscounts. Garbage in, garbage out.*

ER *There are two primary goals that are addressed by regression models in this paper:*
1) general understanding of the data within a given state. In other words identifying variables that aid in a linear prediction of the candidate's vote; and 2) predicting y, given x, for future observations.

RC Which data? The adjusted demographic data or the actual pristine   data?
If Y = f(X), then X should not be forced to fit the recorded result.

ER: *For the purposes of this paper the sample of polling locations using the final end of night results are used as the response variable. Generally for all states past data tends to be a very good predictor of current results. In some states there are other predictors (e.g. precinct boundary changes, current voter registration, weather, etc.) that work well while in other states those same predictors provide no additional information and make the model unnecessarily complex.*

RC But past data does not reflect the prior True Vote, so any regression analysis cannot predict the True Vote. It will however predict the bogus, recorded vote.

ER *Again, the regression model presented here is an example model used for demonstration purposes (i.e. no formal model selection procedure was used). Furthermore, for this same purpose the non-informative prior is used. It's clear from the output of the regression summary that there is a strong effect for 2008 candidate vote percentage, precincts with high Democrat vote in 2008 tend to have a very predictable Democrat vote in 2012. As one would expect the 2012 exit poll results have a strong effect when predicting the final polling location results.*

RC All this is saying that a candidate's vote share is predictable using regression analysis based on the 2008 recorded vote and 2012 adjusted precinct exit poll data. But if the precinct data is biased; the projection will reflect the bias. And the cycle continues in all elections that follow.

ER *We can check to see if the observed data from the polling places are consistent with the fitted model. Based on the model and the predictive distribution, the model fits quite well without outliers in any of the precincts.*

RC Of course the model will fit the bogus recorded vote quite well because it was forced to match the recorded vote. But what if the precinct vote data is manipulated?

ER *Several important conclusions about the analysis of exit poll data can be drawn from this review of approaches using probability distributions. First, it is clear that there are many probability distribution components to an exit poll.*

RC But prior recorded vote and adjusted exit polls in the probability analysis is bogus as long as there is no consideration of the Election Fraud Factor.

ER *This research on exit polling serves as an exploration of ways to investigate and analyze data and to provide alternate, complementary approaches that may be more fully integrated into standard election (and non-election) exit polling. These procedures are only a few of the many ways that can be used to analyze exit poll data. These approaches provide an alternate way to summarize and report on these data. It also provides additional visualization and ways to view the data and how the data are distributed.*

Further topics include small sample sizes, missing data, censored data, and a deeper investigation into absentee/early voting. Additionally, these approaches can be used to investigate various complex sample design techniques (e.g. stratified, cluster, multi-phase, etc.) and evaluate how the designs interact with probabilistic approaches in an exit polling context. Further hierarchical modeling may provide additional insight into the complexities of the exit poll data.

RC: But the core problem is not addressed here. All alternative models are useless if they are based on prior and current recorded vote data which has been corrupted. The pollsters adjust returning voters and/or vote shares to match the recorded vote. They make the invalid assumption that the recorded vote is the true vote. It is an unscientific myth which only serves to perpetuate fraud.

Perspectives on an Exit Poll Reference

My comments in bold follow selected paragraphs from Chapter 1 of a new text *Exit Polls:Surveying the American Electorate, 1972-2010* by Samuel J. Best, University of Connecticut and Brian S. Krueger, University of Rhode Island.

"Despite the unique insights that exit polls can provide about the composition and preferences of voters, they are seldom used after the days immediately following an election. Once media organizations have tapped the exit polls for explanations of electoral outcomes, they often disappear from the public eye. Some scholars may use them over the next year or two to explore the voting behavior of certain subgroups, such as Hispanics, women, or young people, but for the most part they recede into memory, rarely used beyond the next national election."

"Unfortunately, few efforts are made to consider the behavior of voters over time. Historical context typically centers on comparing an election to its most recent predecessor, such as contrasting the 2008 presidential election with the 2004 contest. Rarely are exit poll responses tracked and analyzed over time, leaving many important questions understudied. For example, how have various subgroups in the electorate evolved over time? Have their relative sizes in the active electorate increased or decreased? Have their voting patterns grown increasingly partisan or independent? Which subgroups in the electorate behave similarly through the years?

Of the 274 state exit polls, 232 red-shifted to the Republican. A total of 135 exceeded the margin of error (14 would be expected at the 95% confidence level). Of the 135 polls, an astounding 131 red-shifted to the Republican, proving systemic election fraud beyond any doubt. The probability is ZERO.

"In the weeks and months that follow, exit polls are used time and again to give meaning to the election results. Newly elected officials rely on them to substantiate policy mandates they claim to have received from voters. Partisan pundits scrutinize them for successful and failed campaign strategies. Even political strategists use them to pinpoint key groups and issues that need to be won over to succeed in future elections."

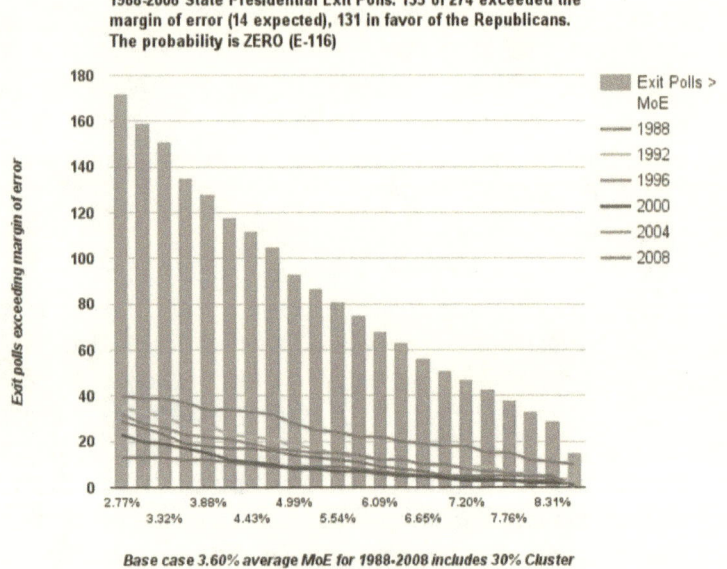

1988-2008 State Presidential Exit Polls: 135 of 274 exceeded the margin of error (14 expected), 131 in favor of the Republicans. The probability is ZERO (E-116)

Base case 3.60% average MoE for 1988-2008 includes 30% Cluster factor (2.77% zero cluster)

But what if the final, adjusted exit polls can be shown to be mathematically impossible? In the 1988, 1992, 2004, 2008 elections, the National Exit Poll had to be adjusted to match the recorded vote. This is standard operating procedure - and very few know of it. But in order to conform to the recorded vote in these four elections, there had to be millions more returning Bush voters than were still living. Obviously, an impossibility.

Therefore, since the national exit polls were adjusted using impossible numbers, this is absolute proof that the recorded vote must also be impossible. Let's look at the 2004 numbers.

The adjusted 2004 National Exit Poll indicated that there were 52.6 million (43% of 122 million recorded votes) returning Bush 2000 voters. But Bush had just 50.5 million recorded votes in 2000. Applying an estimated 5% voter mortality rate, 48 million Bush 2000 voters were living in 2004. Therefore, Bush needed a 110% turnout (52.6/48) turnout of his living 2000 voters to match the 2004 recorded vote, clearly a physical and mathematical impossibility. Assuming 98% turnout, there were only 47 million returning Bush voters. So where did the 5.6 million phantom voters come from?

In fact, Kerry won the unadjusted state and national exit polls. He won the unadjusted state exit poll weighted aggregate of 76,000 respondents by 50.97-47.71%.

UNADJUSTED NATIONAL EXIT POLL (13660 RESPONDENTS)

13660	Kerry	Bush	Other
Sample	7,064	6,414	182
Share	51.71%	46.95%	1.33%

"Unfortunately, these same exit poll results are not easily accessible to members of the public interested in dissecting them. After appearing in the next day's newspapers or on a politically oriented website, they disappear quickly from sight as the election fades in prominence. Eventually, the exit polls are archived at universities where only subscribers are capable of retrieving the data. But nowhere is a complete set of biennial exit poll results available in an easy-to-use format for curious parties."

I created the 1988-2008 state and national presidential exit polls spreadsheet database as an analytical resource using Roper as the data source. This graph summarizes the discrepancies between the exit polls and the recorded votes

"Second, and far more troublesome for the reputation of the exit polls, the preliminary exit poll results showed a partisan skew. They overstated Bill Clinton's share of the vote by 2.5 points in the 1992 presidential race and understated George H. W. Bush's share by 2.5 points, giving the impression that Clinton won by a far greater margin than the officially tabulated votes indicated."

"The raw exit poll data had never been deemed "accurate" in the past prior to being weighted to the actual results, but with the release of early results, observable, but correctable, sampling errors gave the impression that the numbers were off."

One very plausible reason that they were "off" were the 10 million net uncounted votes, the majority from minority precincts that are 90%+ Democratic. The voters were polled, but their votes were not counted. Clinton may have lost millions of other votes due to switched and stuffed ballots. In order to match the 1992 recorded vote, the Final National Exit Poll required that 119% of living Bush 1988 voters turned out in 1992.

"VRS claimed the Democratic overstatement in the raw exit poll data was due to partisan differences in the willingness of voters to complete the exit poll, not to a poor selection of precincts or differential response rates by age, race, or gender. Republicans simply refused to participate at the same rates as Democrats, resulting in there being fewer Republicans in the raw exit poll results than there should have been. Mitofsky speculated that the disparity was due to different intensities of support for the candidates— Democratic voters were just more excited about voting for Clinton than Republican voters were about voting for Bush and, as a result, were more motivated to communicate this message by filling out the

exit poll questionnaire; others thought it was due to Republicans in general having less confidence in the mass media."

Mitofsky may have "speculated" but there is no evidence that Democrats were more responsive to the exit pollsters. In fact, since 2000 response rates in GOP strongholds were higher than comparable Democratic rates. GOP exit poll and vote shares were positively correlated (.25) to state exit poll response. The average Democratic correlation was -0.26. Bush vote shares increased as response rates increased. In 2004, exit poll precinct data showed that response rates were higher in partisan Bush precincts.

"Despite the source of the partisan bias in the raw results, the exit polls were able to characterize accurately the voting patterns of demographic subgroups and partisan constituencies once they were weighted to match the official returns. The problem was that the data could not be corrected until the official results began coming in. As a result, the exit polls were susceptible to inaccurate vote projections on election night, especially early in the evening right after poll closings. Nonetheless, the cautious analysts at VRS still called all the races correctly in the 1992 election."

The data could not be corrected until the official votes came in? Or was it that the data could not be rigged until the official votes came in? Of course the cautious analysts called the winner correctly – Clinton won easily – but they did not call the vote shares correctly. Clinton won by a much bigger margin than they said he did.

The 2000 Election Debacle
"Network competition to call winners culminated in the disastrous 2000 presidential election, when these systems of race projections broke down, and the networks wound up retracting their calls for the winner in Florida and presumptively the election, not once, but twice on election night. The trouble began early in the evening, when VNS

alerted the networks around 7:50 p.m. that their statistical models predicted Al Gore the winner in Florida and that the networks should consider calling the state for Gore. This prediction took place even though only 4 percent of the actual vote had been counted and numerous precincts in the Florida panhandle, which happened to be in the central time zone, remained open until 8 p.m."

If the exit polls show a clear winner - as they did in Florida - the fact that just 4% of the votes were recorded is irrelevant. The exit polls were completed by 7:50pm – and panhandle precincts were exit polled throughout the day. Calling the race 10 minutes before the polls closed was of no consequence. Gore won the Florida exit poll (1816 respondents) by a whopping 53.4-43.6%, far beyond the 3% margin of error.

"Less than ten minutes later, the decision desks at all the networks and the AP agreed with VNS and announced Gore the winner in Florida. Over the next hour-and-a-half, VNS discovered that vote-count data from Duval County had been entered incorrectly, making Gore appear as if he had many more votes than he actually did. After fixing this error, the statistical models used by VNS and decision desks at all the networks showed the race could no longer be projected safely for either candidate. By 10:18 p.m., all the networks announced they were moving the state back to the undecided category, prompting Jeff Greenfield of CNN to quip, "Oh waiter, one order of crow.""

Of the 185,000 spoiled ballots in Florida, 113,000 were double and triple punched – and Gore's name was punched on 75% of them. Almost 30,000 overpunched ballots were in Duval County which has a large black population.

Could the spoiled ballots have been the cause of the Duval adjustments?

"At 2:15 a.m., Fox News called Florida and the presidency for Bush. Within five minutes, NBC, CNN, CBS, and ABC followed suit, announcing that Bush would be the forty-third president of the United States. Meanwhile, VNS and the AP chose not to call the race in Florida a second time, wary of the volatility in the data with the contest that close. During the next couple hours, new errors were discovered. VNS had underestimated the number of votes remaining to be counted. Two counties—Volusia and Brevard—had mistakenly entered their vote totals in favor of Bush. Once these mistakes were corrected, the race narrowed considerably, so much so that Bush's lead was inside the margin of error."

What about the -16,022 Gore votes in Volusia? The media commentators called it a computer "glitch". They always do. They never consider that it could have been the result of malicious coding.

"An embarrassment early in the evening had turned to a humiliation by the end, leading NBC News anchor Tom Brokaw to remark, "We don't just have egg on our face; we have an omelet."

"Despite the resulting indignation, the exit polls were not responsible for the erroneous second call. In fact, the exit polls were at that point no longer part of the estimation models, having been replaced by actual vote counts—incorrect as they were in some cases over the course of the evening."

Replaced by actual vote counts? That is what the perpetrators wanted to do all along. The media never reported that Gore won the unadjusted state exit polls **by 50.8-44.5% (5.5 million votes) - way beyond the MoE. Or that he won the unadjusted National Exit Poll 48.5-46.2%, a 2.5 million margin. There were 5.4 million net uncounted votes. The True Vote Model indicates that he had 50.7%.**

"However, the partisan skew in the measure of aggregate vote

choice was higher than in previous elections. The preliminary data overstated the difference in the George W. Bush-John Kerry vote on election night by 5.5 percentage points, predicting a 51-48-percent advantage for Kerry rather than a 50.5-48 percent win for Bush."

Kerry won the <u>unadjusted state exit poll aggregate</u> by 51.0-47.9%. He won the unadjusted National Exit Poll by 51.7-47.0%. The True Vote Model indicates that he had 53.5%.

"This was the highest error in the preliminary results since the 1992 election and double the error found in the previous two presidential elections. The discrepancy between the preliminary exit poll findings and the final election results was even greater in the competitive states. The exit polls predicted a Kerry victory in four states—Ohio, Iowa, New Mexico, and Nevada—in which Bush won, and overstated Kerry's support by 11 percentage points in Ohio, 9 points in Pennsylvania, and 8 points in Florida."

"Considering the closeness of the election, the exit polls seemed to suggest that Kerry was capable of winning the 2004 election. Political observers used these differences between the preliminary exit polls and the final results to support allegations of vote rigging and fraud in precincts deploying electronic voting machines, particularly in Ohio, where the state's twenty-seven electoral votes, enough to change the winner of the Electoral College from Bush to Kerry, was decided by 118,775 ballots."

The adjusted National Exit Poll indicated that there were 52.6 million returning Bush 2000 voters. But in the 2000 election, Bush had just 50.5 million recorded votes. He needed a 110% turnout of living Bush 2000 voters to match the 2004 recorded vote. Clearly a physical and mathematical impossibility.

"Steven Freeman of the University of Pennsylvania calculated the odds of the exit polls in Ohio, Pennsylvania, and Florida being as far off the final sd 660,000 to 1."

Note: The state exit poll margin of error (MoE) includes a 30% cluster factor.
In Pennsylvania, there were 2107 respondents (2.75% MoE).
Kerry won the poll by 56.6-42.9%, an 800,000 vote margin.

In Ohio, there were 2020 respondents (2.82% MoE).
Kerry won the poll by 54.1-45.7%, a 450,000 vote margin.

In Florida, there were 2862 respondents (2.38% MoE).
Kerry won the poll by 50.8-48.2%, a 200,000 vote margin.

"The National Election Data Archive, a nonpartisan group of mathematicians and statisticians promoting election reform, found that twenty-two of the forty-nine precincts in Ohio polled by Edison/Mitofsky had reported Kerry vote share results that had less than a 5 percent chance of occurring, based on the state's exit polls."

"Rep. John Conyers, D-Mich., even used the exit polls as the basis for holding congressional hearings on vote irregularities in Ohio. Edison/Mitofsky disputed these charges in a follow-up report, contending that precincts with electronic voting had virtually the same rates of error as those using punch card systems."

"They again attributed the bias to within-precinct error—error due to a systematic bias in the selection of voters within a precinct—and not to bias in the selection of precincts themselves. Bush voters were more likely to refuse to participate in the exit polls than Kerry voters. They hypothesized that the result was a function of the disproportionate numbers of interviewers under age thirty-five who administered the exit poll. Young people had more problems securing participation from voters than older respondents, perhaps because they were correctly perceived to have been more likely to have voted for Kerry.

That is the same old discredited and debunked reluctant Bush responder canard that was refuted by the exit pollsters own data which showed that exit poll response was highest in partisan Bush precincts and in strong Republican states.

"Edison/Mitofsky also found that voting patterns within electoral groups were accurate once they were weighted to the official results. They found no evidence that the distribution of presidential vote choices within various demographic groups was biased, despite the vote choice of exit poll respondents overall overstating Democratic support."

The "overstating" of 56 Kerry respondents for every 50 Bush respondents was not due to differential response; it was due to the fact that Kerry won the election with about 53% of the vote.

"Since 2004, less controversy has surrounded the exit polls. No serious technical problems have surfaced during the last three elections, enabling the media to prepare analyses of the outcome in a timely manner. Leaks of early wave findings have been contained. The preliminary exit polls have continued to overstate support for Democratic candidates; however, the final vote counts have had such large winning margins that the projected outcomes were no different."

In 2008, Obama won the recorded vote by 52.9-45.6% - 9.5 million vote margin. But the exit polls indicated that he won by nearly 23 million. The level of fraud was equivalent to 2004. Obama won the aggregate of the unadjusted state exit polls (82,388 respondents) by 58.0-40.5% and the unadjusted National Exit Poll (17,836 respondents) by 61-37%. He had 58% in True Vote Model - exactly matching the state exit polls. How does one explain the massive discrepancy?

"National exit pollsters choose precincts by taking stratified

probability samples in each of the states before drawing a national subsample from the state samples. This process involves sorting the precincts in each state into different categories or strata to guarantee that particular groups are represented adequately. To begin, precincts in each state are initially grouped into two strata according to their size to ensure the selection of smaller precincts."

"Within each of these size strata, precincts are categorized by geographic region, usually between three to five regions in each state. For each state geographic region, precincts are ordered by their percentage vote for one of the major political parties in a previous election. Precincts are sampled from these strata with probabilities proportionate to the total votes cast in them in a prior election, so that every precinct has as many chances of being picked by pollsters as it has voters. The samples drawn in each state are then combined, and a national sample of precincts is selected from them using a previous presidential race to determine the relative number of precincts chosen from each state."

Sampling voters in proportion to the recorded vote in prior elections is a persistent source of bias, since the recorded votes were fraudulent and favored the Republicans. So the sampled exit polled precincts were over-weighted for the GOP.

"Typically, the total number of precincts selected in the national exit poll is between 250 and 300. Ultimately, the number of precincts chosen represents a tradeoff between sampling error and financial constraints. Research by Edison/Mitofsky has shown that the number of precincts selected has not been responsible for the Democratic overstatements that have continually appeared in the exit polls."

"For example, they found that for the 2004 election the actual distribution of the presidential vote in the precincts used in the exit poll samples did not differ significantly from the actual vote distribution nationwide. In fact, these precincts overstated support for

the Republican candidate, George W. Bush, but only by 0.4 points, on average, across the states."

Mitofsky claimed that the precinct samples were perfect. He also hypothesized that 56 Democrats responded for every 50 Republicans – even though his own data indicates that response rates were higher in partisan Bush precincts.

"Refusal rates, or for that matter miss rates, are not necessarily problematic, as long as the propensity of different groups to participate does not vary. However, if one group is more or less likely than other groups to complete exit surveys, their responses will be over or under-represented, thereby biasing estimates for the overall electorate. For example, the partisan overstatement repeatedly found in the national exit polls over the past several decades appears to be due to the greater willingness of Democratic voters to complete the exit polls, compared with their Republican counterparts. However, once this discrepancy has been corrected by weighting the exit polls to correspond with the actual vote, there has been no evidence that the vote estimates within groups are biased."

In 2000, 2004 and 2008, GOP exit polls and vote shares were positively correlated (0.25) to exit poll response. US Count Votes comprehensive analysis of the 2004 exit poll discrepancies disproved the exit pollster's reluctant Bush responder hypothesis.

"National exit pollsters account for early/absentee voting by conducting telephone surveys in states where the rates of early voting are highest. VNS first incorporated early/absentee voting in 1996, surveying voters in California, Oregon, Texas, and Washington. By 2008, NEP was conducting telephone surveys in eighteen states, including Oregon, Washington, and Colorado, where the proportions of early voting were so high that no in-person exit polls were conducted on Election Day."

Early voting data in the 2008 election indicates that Oregon, Washington, and Colorado had the lowest red-shifts. Was it just a coincidence that the states with the highest early voting rates most closely matched the unadjusted exit polls?

6. Summary Analysis

The authors, both engineers, referred to my work and that of other election integrity analysts in this excellent article: *Just Doing the Math: Electoral Fraud in the 2016 Democratic Primaries* By Giovanni and Marcello Pietrobon

http://democracyintegrity.org/index.html

Synopsis

After delving into the investigations of mathematician and numerical control engineer Richard Charnin, FBI journalist investigator Greg Palast and election investigator and analyst Bev Harris, an Italian observer of American politics becomes persuaded not only that statistical methods can show when fraud has taken place, but that in fact the American electoral system is structured to allow it and hide it. He unpacks some statistical concepts to explain this to his brother, a naturalized American, and he in turn passes the information to us.

My brother Marcello and I have been talking about electoral irregularities for months. He's an astronomer by training, a software engineer, and an avid follower of American politics. I'm a microelectronic engineer and a finance person living in the United States for the past 20 years. As Italians we both look at American politics with a great deal of curiosity and sometimes disbelief. As a naturalized American, I worry.

Recently, Marcello became interested in the sort of calculation that could actually detect electoral fraud having heard about so many indications of electoral rigging in these past democratic primaries. After delving into the investigations of mathematician and numerical control engineer Richard Charnin, FBI journalist investigator Greg Palast[1], and election investigator and analyst Bev Harris[2], among others, he is persuaded not only that statistical methods can show when fraud has taken place, but that in fact the American electoral system is structured to allow it and to hide it[3]. He spent a few days unpacking a few statistical concepts for me regarding this proposition and I will try to convey them to you.

First we should be aware that exit polls, the polls of voters taken immediately after they have exited the polling stations, are the only way to check against fraud in elections while keeping the vote confidential. A discrepancy between the declared vote (recorded vote) and the vote extrapolated from the exit polls is an indication of fraud when it is above a margin of error of 2% within a confidence level of 95%.

Here is how it works. When statisticians try to measure the 'real vote' they not only estimate the final vote count but they also analyze the entire distribution of the data they gathered from the exit poll voter sampling in order to determine the reliability of their final determination. When fluctuations in the data are due to randomness they will follow a statistical distribution that follows the shape of a bell curve, the Gaussian curve. The reliability or unreliability of the sample data doesn't depend so much on the trustworthiness of those who collect the exit poll voter sampling, but it's rather intrinsic to the shape of the distribution. From this shape an 'interval of confidence' is determined within which we can unquestionably claim our confidence that we got it right with a probability of 95% — always 95%. This interval of confidence is also called 'margin of error' (MoE).

Poorly informed 'experts' frequently argue that the statistical analysis of exit polls can be misleading because it assumes that real life data is randomly distributed (as in the Gaussian curve) when that's not always the case. And here is where they are missing a central point. The expectation that sample data will be randomly distributed ALREADY takes into account all possible relevant factors in a practical observation in real life. When extraneous factors intervene, a discrepancy will make the recorded value fall outside of the interval of confidence signaling only one possibility: a systematic error. When this occurs statisticians make further analysis to determine the causes, and either remove the cause or include it into the 'margin of error'. After 59 years of fine-tuning this process in countless elections around the world statisticians have reached a point where exit polls have become extremely reliable. If the final 'Recorded Vote' falls outside the interval of confidence one can assume with a high degree of certainty that the systematic error is intentional. This is why we say that we have a high probability of fraud.

The fact that such a high probability of fraud is so apparent in the comparison of exit polls and recorded vote is partially masked by the way electoral results are obtained in the United States. The results of most democratic elections around the world are obtained with a 95% confidence level within a margin of error of 2%. In fact, these are the parameters that the U.S. government normally uses to oversee elections in other countries (https://en.wikipedia.org/wiki/List_of_controversial_elections).

But this is **not true in the U.S itself** — which nobody thinks of supervising.

Election results in the United States are obtained with a 95% confidence level within a **3-4% margin of error**. This is because relatively recent laws in the United States have intentionally rendered reference data less reliable (HAVA, Bush 2002). By law exit polls must be adjusted to match the final recorded vote, which means that evidence of fraud is suppressed. Exit poll results, already partially manipulated, must disappear after a given election and become public only 5 years later. When such data has become available in its unadjusted complete form, it has been used to cross-check voting results with other independent methods. The results have not only shown that the numbers were internally coherent but also that they corroborated original suspicions of fraud.

In the 2016 democratic primary elections unadjusted exit polls show that Bernie Sanders has been robbed of the following percentage of votes: Alabama 6.1%, Arizona 22.1%, Georgia 5.5%, Massachusetts 4.0%, Mississippi 4.7%, Ohio 5.0%, South Carolina 5.2%, Texas 4.2%, Wisconsin 6.9%, West Virginia 6.0%, New York 5.9% (CNN

New York exit polls indicated that Bernie Sanders may have done better than 48% there).

Although a discrepancy of -4.6% in Oklahoma turned out to be in favor of Bernie, it doesn't affect our analysis[4] because so far the discrepancies shown in all of the above final results have been consistently larger than the MoE in favor of Hillary in 11 of the 26 primaries. The probability of this happening without fraud is 1 in 77 billion (6.8-sigma). In other words, one can expect something this improbable to happen less than once since the extinction of dinosaurs — if elections were to be a daily event.

Exit polls discrepancies: 24 out of 26 are in Hillary's favor exceeding the margin of error in 11 primaries.

The probability P of this happening is 1 in 77 billion.

One can also search for trends to check for fraud. One of the most revealing methods, the Cumulative Vote Share Analysis, searches for a correlation between the size of a discrepancy (between recorded vote and exit polls) and the size of a precinct. When no fraud has taken place the trend tends to be quite regular. When the discrepancy tends to manifest as the size of the precinct becomes larger than a certain value, it is a strong indication of fraud, according to Richard Charnin. Roughly speaking the reason for this behavior is that electronic rigging is implemented strategically in order not to become obvious. The discrepancy caused by the rigging is "better" distributed between those precincts that are big enough to be worth the effort.

Above a certain precinct size the vote share increases in favor of one candidate. There should be no correlation, like we see on the diagram on the left (Utah).

In fact, in the recent democratic primaries we can observe a noticeable divergence in trends between the Clinton and Sanders votes when the precincts are larger; the larger the size, the higher the percentage of the votes that go in favor of Clinton. This has been evident in Massachusetts (>10%), Michigan (>3%-10% according to the type of machines), Missouri (>0.05% the size is small but the trend unequivocal), New York (>10% and possibly >20%). Charnin's diagrams (see below) are self-explanatory.

In Kentucky Hillary's cumulative vote share increased by 7.4% (55.9% to 63.3%) after 85% of the smaller precincts were counted! The probability P of this vote spike occurring by chance is essentially ZERO.

All in all electoral anomalies have been apparent in New York, Massachusetts, Illinois, Arizona, Iowa, Nevada, Ohio, Delaware, Wyoming, Wisconsin, Missouri, Michigan, Alabama, Tennessee, Georgia, Arkansas, Texas, Kentucky and Oregon. But electoral fraud has been particularly evident in strategic elections such as those in Arizona and New York. They were meant to kill the Bernie Sander's momentum. And they did just that with the help of the media.

Disenfranchisement — widespread in New York and Arizona — has been more widely reported so I will not discuss it here. But in any case it must be added to other forms of electoral fraud.

According to the recorded vote the Sanders-Clinton competition is currently at 43.5-56.5% with a lead of 3 million votes in favor of Clinton. But actual votes in caucus states have not been included, and the fact that unadjusted exit polls have indicated that voting machines were hacked has not been considered. According to Charnin, if we take this into account we would have Sanders at 47.9 and Clinton at 52.1%, with a lead of 1.3 million votes in favor of Clinton. Furthermore, if we also take into consideration that voter rolls were manipulated and that long lines and severely shortened polling station hours reduced voter turnout in areas favorable to Sanders, we would need to add a 10% to Sanders's votes and subtract 5% from Clinton's. That would put Sanders in the lead at 51.5-48.5% (780,000 votes) in his favor.[5]

Sanders's supporters have barely begun to speak about electoral irregularities and already the DNC has started to accuse them and Sander's campaign of inciting "violence" among supporters by promoting allegations that the primary process is rigged in favor of his opponent, Hillary Clinton.[6]

There's much more to say. This is only a piece of the larger story of how fraud has become part and parcel of American elections, which has been at work since the 1960s, reaching extraordinary highs after the year 2000. Most notable have been the elections stolen from Al Gore by 6 million votes, from Kerry by more than 10 million and the landslide vote margins stolen from Obama both in 2008 and 2012. But if until now the biggest share of electoral rigging has come from the Republicans by far, it looks like the Democrats are more than willing to step up to the plate if an uncorrupt candidate dares to challenge their establishment. Berkeley, June 3rd, 2016

[1] Palast is not in U.S. now because he says 'investigative journalism has become illegal after the Patriot Act III. www.gregpalast.com

[2] Bev Harris sent Diebold to court and discovered that in the U.S. people vote by fractions, like 0.70 or 1.3, not just by a simple integer which should be always 1.http://blackboxvoting.org/fraction-magic-1/

[3] For more a comedic take on electoral fraud in 2016 watch comedian and activist Lee Camp at Redacted Tonight. https://www.youtube.com/channel/UCyvaZ2RHEDrgKXz43gz7CbQ

[4] Cyber Theft Expert Jonathan Simon has explained the OK anomaly. Seehttp://www.opednews.com/articles/Jonathan-Simon-Election-C-by-Joan-Brunwasser-2016-Presidential-Election_2016-Presidential-Primary-Candidates_Election-Fraud_Election-Integrity-160521-727.html

[5] richardcharnin.wordpress.com

[6] http://www.opednews.com/articles/Sanders-Scolded-For-Callin-by-Kevin-Gosztola-Bernie-Sanders-2016-Presidential-Candidate_DNC-Chairman_Democrats-DNC_Wasserman-Schultz-Debbie-160521-905.html

7. Voting Systems

Current voting systems are designed to be hacked. We need systems that are designed to work. It's that simple. Systems designed by experts that employ data redundancy, auditable processes, open source code which are non-proprietary and allow voters to confirm their precinct vote.

As computer security expert Steve Spoonamore has said: you just need to make sure that 1+1=2. It's not rocket science. If voters have the ability to check their vote after it has been transmitted to a tabulator and find a mistake, they can report it. It is a citizen auditable process. Spoonamore is allowed to analyze Diebold ATM software, but prohibited from looking at Diebold's voting machine code. He agrees that Open Source is an appropriate solution. He calls it "freeware".

Posters who claim that technology can never guarantee that elections and that any system can be hacked. But they fail to consider that technology, used in conjunction with low-tech hand-counts, provides a more secure voting system than hand-counts alone. There would be an additional benefit: election officials could not install unverifiable machines that have consistently failed inspection procedures.

The public should own the voting hardware and software. Each voter should be able to check his/her vote. We need a hybrid system of hand-counted ballot summaries posted for viewing at the precinct as well as on the Internet. Each ballot contains an anonymous voter code so voters can check their votes online. It is a self-auditing system which is data redundant and transparent. Only an Open Source/Internet system can provide a solution. Diebold and ES&S voting machines and central tabulators use proprietary code for one reason only: they are designed to be manipulated. Non-proprietary hardware and software is the solution.

The use of current closed, vulnerable systems by election officials and their refusal to consider an Open Source solution is proof that it would work. Voters would have online access to their vote. They would in effect be auditing and exit polling themselves.

Open Source skeptics believe that the solution is hand-counting the ballots at the voting site. But this is only a partial solution. The precinct votes must be tabulated. The other requirement is uploading the precinct data to an Internet-based Open Source system which can be voter-verified.

The technology skeptics claim that technology is incapable of insuring fair elections and that every system can be hacked. They fail to consider that the primary goal of any security system is data redundancy, transparency and built-in safeguards to detect fraud.

Computer experts want fair elections. Why not create a prototype? Refusal to even consider that Open Source could enhance hand-counting ballots only serves to enable the corruption. But what if the experts can provide such a hybrid solution? Would they accept it?

Open Source: Sanders Landslide in Humboldt County

In California, just ONE county uses an Open Source System to audit and count votes. Could that be why Bernie had 71% of the 2-party vote in Humboldt County? It was his highest vote share in ALL 58 counties! The system is a deterrent to fraud. View the 58 California counties: Election Day and post-Election Day votes.

The Humboldt Open Source (TEVS) tabulation system was pioneered in 2006 by Mitch Trachtenberg, a computer programmer, together with Carolyn Crnich, registrar of Humboldt County and Kevin Collins, election integrity activist. The election showed significant problems in the Diebold system they were using in counting votes.

As result of these problems, Diebold abruptly severed its business relationship with Humboldt. Crnich switched to another voting company, Hart InterCivic, but kept the TEVS system functioning. TEVS is the ONLY OPEN SOURCE, TRANSPARENT SYSTEM FOR COUNTING VOTES IN THE UNITED STATES. It is being used as a recounting system to double-check the vote-counting of the Hart InterCivic system which has been performing well, unlike the Diebold system used previously. At the time she introduced TEVS, Carolyn purchased a high speed scanner that could operate independently of any voting machine to tabulate the votes using TEVS.

Bernie's vote share increased over his Election Day share in every county.http://vote.sos.ca.gov/returns/president/party/democratic/county/humboldt/

The Humboldt (CA) County Election Transparency Project (ETP) is a documented case in which technology uncovered vote miscounts. Volunteers scanned ballots after the election to verify the integrity of the Diebold/Premier machines. The images were made publicly available and used TEVs ballot counting software .http://code.google.com/p/tevs/

They found that 197 ballots were deleted by the Diebold/Premier GEMS software used by Humboldt County to tally the vote. This software glitch resulted in the certification of inaccurate election results. The Election Administration Research Center at UC Berkeley site contains ballot images that were scanned during this project (the same images can also be obtained on DVD from the Elections Office).The ballot extraction code reads the ballot image and uses OCR to automatically determine the candidates listed on the ballot. It reads the images and stores the results in a database.

The ETP is overseen by officials from the Humboldt County Elections Office. However, the "elbow grease" of this project, with a couple of exceptions, is done by volunteers who care about the integrity of our elections. These volunteers, working on weekends, holidays, and evenings, use a high-end office scanner to scan all paper ballots cast in an election. The scanner produces digital images of the ballots. The ballots are "digitally signed" to mark their authenticity and uploaded to the Internet for distribution. These images are also available on DVD at the Elections Office. One notable feature is that each ballot is imprinted with a unique serial number before it is imaged. Part of the serial number contains information about on the box the ballot comes from. This feature "ties together" an image on the Internet with the paper ballot.

A site belonging to ETP volunteer Mitch Trachtenberg contains an Open Source software program that automates the counting of these ballot images. This auditing tool is quite valuable in producing a tally that can be used to compare against the results produced by software that is not subject to inspection by members of the general public. In short, this tool alleviates the need of counting ballots by hand and does so in a transparent manner.

Is it just a coincidence that Bernie Sanders had his best vote share (71%) in Humboldt County, CA, the only county in the U.S. which has an Open Source audit/vote count system?
Humboldt County in California implemented an Open Source vote counting and auditing system. It is the only Open Source system in the U.S. Is it just a coincidence that Bernie Sanders had his highest vote share (71%) in Humboldt?

Skeptics avoid the Open Source solution. How can they be so sure that it would never work? Corrupt election officials will not be able to rig Open Source systems with hand-counted paper ballots designed by experts in computer security and software design. How can the claim that non-proprietary, robust hardware/software based election systems would never work? The fault lies not in our technology, but in our failure to apply it to make our election vote counting fraud-free.

8. Adjusted Exit Polls

Democratic primary exit polls were adjusted to match the recorded vote to within 0.06%. The average of the adjusted exit poll discrepancies from the recorded vote is virtually zero - a perfect match. Unadjusted exit polls are always forced to match the recorded vote. The premise is that there is ZERO fraud in every election polled.

The Gender crosstab is the basis for calculating adjusted vote shares. Exit poll naysayers proclaim that the polls are not designed to forecast a winner. But males and females are asked who they just voted for. Isn't that the same thing as forecasting the winner?

CT	1234	Resp	MoE	3.63%				
Final		Clinton	Sanders	Other		Clinton	Sanders	Other
Men	39%	43%	55%	2%		25%	70%	5%
Women	61%	55%	41%	4%		50%	46%	4%
	Total	50.32%	46.46%	3.22%		40.25%	55.36%	4.39%
	2-party	51.99%	48.01%			42.10%	57.90%	
	Recorded	51.80%	46.40%	1.80%		51.80%	46.40%	1.80%
	Diff	-1.48%	0.06%	1.42%		-11.55%	8.96%	2.59%
	Discrepancy	5.53%			Discrepancy	-20.51%		

MD	1364	Resp	MoE	3.33%				
		Clinton	Sanders	Other		Clinton	Sanders	Other
Men	39%	55%	40%	5%		55%	40%	5%
Women	61%	68%	29%	3%		68%	29%	3%
	Total	62.93%	33.29%	3.78%		62.93%	33.29%	3.78%
	2-party	65.40%	34.60%			65.40%	34.60%	
	Recorded	65.50%	34.50%	0.00%		65.50%	34.50%	0.00%
	Diff	-2.57%	-1.21%	3.78%		-2.57%	-1.21%	3.78%
	Discrepancy	-1.36%			Discrepancy	-1.36%		

PA	1425	Resp	MoE	3.35%			
		Clinton	Sanders	Other	Clinton	Sanders	Other
Men	40%	49%	50%	1%	48%	51%	1%
Women	60%	60%	39%	1%	58%	41%	1%
	Total	55.60%	43.40%	1.00%	54.00%	45.00%	1.00%
	2-party	56.16%	43.84%		54.55%	45.45%	
	Recorded	56.10%	43.90%	0.00%	56.10%	43.90%	0.00%
	Diff	-0.50%	-0.50%	1.00%	-2.10%	1.10%	1.00%
	Discrepancy	0.00%			Discrepancy	-3.20%	

IN	1324	Resp	MoE	3.50%		
		Clinton	Sanders		Clinton	Sanders
Men	41%	43%	57%		40%	60%
Women	59%	50%	50%		48%	52%
	Total	47.13%	52.87%		44.72%	55.28%
	2-party	47.13%	52.87%		44.72%	55.28%
	Recorded	47.51%	52.49%		47.51%	52.49%
	Diff	-0.38%	0.38%		-2.79%	2.79%
	Discrepancy	-0.76%			Discrepancy	-5.58%

AL	865	Resp	MoE 3.63%					
		Clinton	Sanders	Other		Clinton	Sanders	Other
Men	40%	73%	24%	3%		66%	31%	3%
Women	60%	80%	17%	3%		74%	23%	3%
	Total	77.20%	19.80%	3.00%		70.80%	26.20%	3.00%
	2-party	79.59%	20.41%			72.99%	27.01%	
	Recorded	77.84%	19.19%	2.97%		77.84%	19.19%	2.97%
	Diff	-0.64%	0.61%	0.03%		-7.04%	7.01%	0.03%
		Discrepancy	-1.25%		Discrepancy	-14.05%		

R	944	Resp	MoE 3.83%					
		Clinton	Sanders	Other		Clinton	Sanders	Other
Men	43%	60%	37%	3%		56%	41%	3%
Women	57%	76%	23%	1%		71%	28%	1%
	Total	69.12%	29.02%	1.86%		64.55%	33.59%	1.86%
	2-party	70.43%	29.57%			65.77%	34.23%	
	Recorded	66.21%	29.74%	4.05%		66.21%	29.74%	4.05%
	Diff	2.91%	-0.72%	-2.19%		-1.66%	3.85%	-2.19%
		Discrepancy	3.63%		Discrepancy	-5.51%		

FL	1659	Resp	MoE	2.99%				
		Clinton	Sanders	Other		Clinton	Sanders	Other
Men	42%	57%	40%	3%		55%	42%	3%
Women	58%	70%	28%	2%		68%	30%	2%
	Total	64.54%	33.04%	2.42%		62.54%	35.04%	2.42%
	2-party	66.14%	33.86%			64.09%	35.91%	
	Recorded	64.50%	33.80%	1.70%		64.50%	33.80%	1.70%
	Diff	0.04%	-0.76%	0.72%		-1.96%	1.24%	0.72%
	Discrepancy	0.80%			Discrepancy	-3.20%		

GA	1491	Resp	MoE	2.96%				
		Clinton	Sanders	Other		Clinton	Sanders	Other
Men	38%	66%	33%	1%		60%	39%	1%
Women	62%	76%	23%	1%		68%	31%	1%
	Total	72.20%	26.80%	1.00%		64.96%	34.04%	1.00%
	2-party	72.93%	27.07%			65.62%	34.38%	
	Recorded	71.33%	28.16%	0.51%		71.33%	28.16%	0.51%
	Diff	0.87%	1.36%	0.49%		-6.37%	5.88%	0.49%
	Discrepancy	2.23%			Discrepancy	-12.25%		

IL	1521	Resp	MoE	3.27%					
		Clinton	Sanders	Other		Clinton	Sanders	Other	
Men	46%	45%	53%	2%		44%	54%	2%	
Women	54%	55%	45%	0%		52%	48%	0%	
	Total	50.40%	48.68%	0.92%		48.32%	50.76%	0.92%	
	2-party	50.87%	49.13%			48.77%	51.23%		
	Recorded	50.46%	48.72%	0.82%		50.46%	48.72%	0.82%	
	Diff	-0.06%	-0.04%	0.10%		-2.14%	2.04%	0.10%	
	Discrepancy		-0.02%		Discrepancy		-4.18%		

IN	1324	Resp	MoE	3.50%				
		Clinton	Sanders			Clinton	Sanders	
Men	41%	43%	57%			40%	60%	
Women	59%	50%	50%			48%	52%	
	Total	47.13%	52.87%			44.72%	55.28%	
	2-party	47.13%	52.87%			44.72%	55.28%	
	Recorded	47.51%	52.49%			47.51%	52.49%	
	Diff	-0.38%	0.38%			-2.79%	2.79%	
	Discrepancy		-0.76%		Discrepancy		-5.58%	

MA	1406	Resp	MoE	3.40%				
		Clinton	Sanders	Other		Clinton	Sanders	Other
Men	42%	41%	57%	2%		38%	60%	2%
Women	58%	58%	42%	0%		52%	48%	0%
	Total	50.86%	48.30%	0.84%		46.12%	53.04%	0.84%
	2-party	51.29%	48.71%			46.51%	53.49%	
	Recorded	50.11%	48.69%	1.20%		50.11%	48.69%	1.20%
	Diff	0.75%	-0.39%	-0.36%		-3.99%	4.35%	-0.36%
	Discrepancy	1.14%			Discrepancy	-8.34%		

MI	1601	Resp	MoE	3.18%				
		Clinton	Sanders	Other		Clinton	Sanders	Other
Men	45%	44%	55%	1%		42%	57%	1%
Women	55%	51%	45%	4%		48%	48%	4%
	Total	47.85%	49.50%	2.65%		45.30%	52.05%	2.65%
	2-party	49.15%	50.85%			46.53%	53.47%	
	Recorded	48.27%	49.83%	1.90%		48.27%	49.83%	1.90%
	Diff	-0.42%	-0.33%	0.75%		-2.97%	2.22%	0.75%
	Discrepancy	-0.09%			Discrepancy	-5.19%		

MO	1168	Resp	MoE	3.73%				
		Clinton	Sanders	Other		Clinton	Sanders	Other
Men	45%	44%	56%	0%		42%	58%	0%
Women	55%	54%	44%	2%		52%	46%	2%
	Total	49.50%	49.40%	1.10%		47.50%	51.40%	1.10%
	2-party	50.05%	49.95%			48.03%	51.97%	
	Recorded	49.60%	49.40%	1.00%		49.60%	49.40%	1.00%
	Diff	-0.10%	0.00%	0.10%		-2.10%	2.00%	0.10%
	Discrepancy	-0.10%			Discrepancy	-4.10%		

MS	1038	Resp	MoE	2.98%				
		Clinton	Sanders	Other		Clinton	Sanders	Other
Men	36%	79%	19%	2%		74%	24%	2%
Women	64%	85%	15%	0%		80%	20%	0%
	Total	82.84%	16.44%	0.72%		77.84%	21.44%	0.72%
	2-party	83.44%	16.56%			78.40%	21.60%	
	Recorded	82.63%	16.46%	0.91%		82.63%	16.46%	0.91%
	Diff	0.21%	-0.02%	-0.19%		-4.79%	4.98%	-0.19%
	Discrepancy	0.23%			Discrepancy	-9.77%		

NC 1867 Resp MoE 2.93%

		Clinton	Sanders	Other		Clinton	Sanders	Other
Men	42%	49%	47%	4%		49%	47%	4%
Women	58%	59%	37%	4%		58%	38%	4%
Total		54.80%	41.20%	4.00%		54.22%	41.78%	4.00%
2-party		57.08%	42.92%			56.48%	43.52%	
Recorded		54.60%	40.80%	4.60%		54.60%	40.80%	4.60%
Diff		0.20%	0.40%	-0.60%		-0.38%	0.98%	-0.60%
Discrepancy		-0.20%				-1.36%		

NH 2222 Resp MoE 2.63%

		Clinton	Sanders	Other		Clinton	Sanders	Other
Men	45%	32%	67%	1%		34%	65%	1%
Women	55%	44%	55%	1%		44%	55%	1%
Total		38.60%	60.40%	1.00%		39.50%	59.50%	1.00%
2-party		38.99%	61.01%			39.90%	60.10%	
Recorded		38.00%	60.40%	1.60%		38.00%	60.40%	1.60%
Diff		0.60%	0.00%	-0.60%		1.50%	-0.90%	-0.60%
Discrepancy		0.60%				2.40%		

NY	1391	Resp	MoE	3.38%		Clinton	Sanders
		Clinton	Sanders			Clinton	Sanders
Men	41%	50%	50%			46%	54%
Women	59%	63%	37%			56%	44%
	Total	57.67%	42.33%			51.90%	48.10%
	2-party	57.67%	42.33%			51.90%	48.10%
	Recorded	57.99%	42.01%			57.99%	42.01%
	Diff	-0.32%	0.32%			-6.09%	6.09%
	Discrepancy		-0.64%		Discrepancy		-12.18%

OH	1764	Resp	MoE	3.01%			Clinton	Sanders	Other
		Clinton	Sanders	Other			Clinton	Sanders	Other
Men	44%	48%	51%	1%			44%	55%	1%
Women	56%	63%	36%	1%			57%	42%	1%
	Total	56.40%	42.60%	1.00%			51.28%	47.72%	1.00%
	2-party	56.97%	43.03%				51.80%	48.20%	
	Recorded	56.50%	42.10%	1.40%			56.50%	42.10%	1.40%
	Diff	-0.10%	0.50%	-0.40%			-5.22%	5.62%	-0.40%
	Discrepancy		-0.60%			Discrepancy		-10.84%	

OK	821	Resp	MoE	4.38%				
		Clinton	Sanders	Other		Clinton	Sanders	Other
Men	46%	33%	60%	7%		38%	55%	7%
Women	54%	48%	46%	6%		51%	43%	6%
	Total	41.10%	52.44%	6.46%		45.02%	48.52%	6.46%
	2-party	43.94%	56.06%			48.13%	51.87%	
	Recorded	41.52%	51.85%	6.63%		41.52%	51.85%	6.63%
	Diff	-0.42%	0.59%	-0.17%		3.50%	-3.33%	-0.17%
	Discrepancy	-1.01%			Discrepancy	6.83%		

SC	1461	Resp	MoE	2.90%			
		Clinton	Sanders			Clinton	Sanders
Men	39%	68%	32%			56%	44%
Women	61%	79%	21%			77%	23%
	Total	74.71%	25.29%			68.81%	31.19%
	2-party	74.71%	25.29%			68.81%	31.19%
	Recorded	73.50%	26.00%			73.50%	26.00%
	Diff	1.21%	-0.71%			-4.69%	5.19%
	Discrepancy	1.92%			Discrepancy	-9.88%	

TN	966	Resp	MoE	3.84%				
		Clinton	Sanders	Other		Clinton	Sanders	Other
Men	42%	64%	35%	1%		58%	41%	1%
Women	58%	70%	29%	1%		66%	33%	1%
	Total	67.48%	31.52%	1.00%		62.64%	36.36%	1.00%
	2-party	68.16%	31.84%			63.27%	36.73%	
	Recorded	66.11%	32.43%	1.46%		66.11%	32.43%	1.46%
	Diff	1.37%	-0.91%	-0.46%		-3.47%	3.93%	-0.46%
	Discrepancy	2.28%			Discrepancy	-7.40%		

TX	1481	Resp	MoE	3.13%				
		Clinton	Sanders	Other		Clinton	Sanders	Other
Men	42%	61%	38%	1%		54%	45%	1%
Women	58%	70%	28%	2%		65%	33%	2%
	Total	66.22%	32.20%	1.58%		60.38%	38.04%	1.58%
	2-party	67.28%	32.72%			61.35%	38.65%	
	Recorded	65.20%	33.20%	1.60%		65.20%	33.20%	1.60%
	Diff	1.02%	-1.00%	-0.02%		-4.82%	4.84%	-0.02%
	Discrepancy	2.02%			Discrepancy	-9.66%		

VA	1413	Resp	MoE	3.25%				
		Clinton	Sanders	Other		Clinton	Sanders	Other
Men	43%	57%	42%	1%		54%	45%	1%
Women	57%	70%	30%	0%		68%	32%	0%
	Total	64.41%	35.16%	0.43%		61.98%	37.59%	0.43%
	2-party	64.69%	35.31%			62.25%	37.75%	
	Recorded	64.29%	35.19%	0.52%		64.29%	35.19%	0.52%
	Diff	0.12%	-0.03%	-0.09%		-2.31%	2.40%	-0.09%
	Discrepancy		0.15%		Discrepancy		-4.71%	

VT	1542	Resp	MoE	2.22%			
		Clinton	Sanders			Clinton	Sanders
Men	43%	9%	91%			8%	92%
Women	57%	17%	83%			17%	83%
	Total	13.56%	86.44%			13.13%	86.87%
	2-party	13.56%	86.44%			13.13%	86.87%
	Recorded	13.62%	86.10%			13.62%	86.10%
	Diff	-0.06%	0.34%			-0.49%	0.77%
	Discrepancy		-0.40%		Discrepancy		-1.26%

WI — 1774 — Resp — MoE 2.99%

		Clinton	Sanders	Other		Clinton	Sanders	Other
Men	43%	35%	64%	1%		32%	67%	1%
Women	57%	49%	50%	1%		42%	57%	1%
Total		42.98%	56.02%	1.00%		37.70%	61.30%	1.00%
2-party		43.41%	56.59%			38.08%	61.92%	
Recorded		43.11%	56.57%	0.32%		43.11%	56.57%	0.32%
Diff		-0.13%	-0.55%	0.68%		-5.41%	4.73%	0.68%
	Discrepancy	0.42%			Discrepancy	-10.14%		

WV — 763 — Resp — MoE 4.42%

		Clinton	Sanders	Other		Clinton	Sanders	Other
Men	47%	34%	53%	13%		33%	62%	5%
Women	53%	37%	50%	13%		39%	57%	4%
Total		35.59%	51.41%	13.00%		36.18%	59.35%	4.47%
2-party		40.91%	59.09%			37.87%	62.13%	
Recorded		35.83%	51.39%	12.78%		35.83%	51.39%	12.78%
Diff		-0.24%	0.02%	0.22%		0.35%	7.96%	-8.31%
	Discrepancy	-0.26%			Discrepancy	-7.61%		

9. 2016 Presidential Election Model

The Election Model estimates plausible state vote shares and calculates the electoral vote assuming a 4-way race between Clinton, Trump, Stein and Johnson. It is not a forecast. It is meant to illustrate a possible scenario given certain assumptions of Party-ID and corresponding vote shares. Independents voted heavily for Sanders.

The model is flexible so that one easily change input vote shares and the Party-ID split. State vote shares and electoral votes are automatically calculated. In 2014, the National Party ID split was: 41% Democrat, 35% Republican and 24% Independent. Current surveys indicate that the current split is 29D-21R-50I – a sharp increase in self-identified Independents.

Methodology

1-State 2016 Party-ID is adjusted proportionate to the change in National Party ID from 2014. For example, Illinois 2014 Party-ID (47D-35R-18I) was adjusted to 40.6D-24.8R-34.6I.
2- National Party-ID vote shares are applied to the state Party-ID split.
3-The total Electoral vote is calculated.

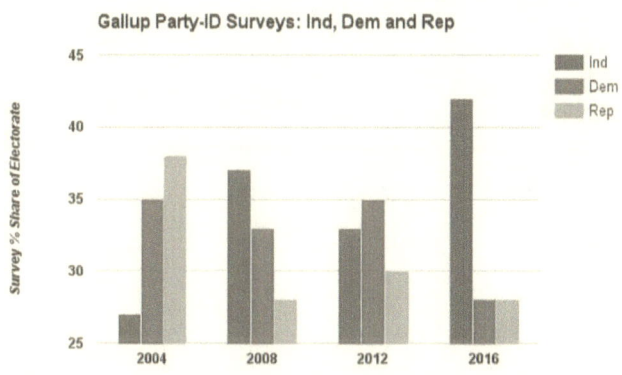

Assumption: Jill Stein performs as well as Bernie Sanders

Party-ID	Pct	Stein	Clinton	Trump	Johnson
Ind	39%	55%	25%	10%	10%
Dem	36%	20%	50%	5%	25%
Rep	25%	5%	5%	75%	15%
Total	100%	29.90%	29.00%	24.45%	16.65%
Votes	129,106	38,603	37,441	31,566	21,496
Elect Vote	538	237	184	117	0

Sensitivity Analysis

Stein % Democrats

Stein % of Ind	16.0%	18.0%	20.0%	22.0%	24.0%
			Stein		
60%	30.4%	31.1%	31.9%	32.6%	33.3%
55%	28.5%	29.2%	29.90%	30.6%	31.3%
50%	26.5%	27.2%	28.0%	28.7%	29.4%
			Clinton		
60%	28.5%	27.8%	27.1%	26.3%	25.6%
55%	30.4%	29.7%	29.00%	28.3%	27.6%
50%	32.4%	31.7%	31.0%	30.2%	29.5%
			Margin		
60%	1.9%	3.4%	4.8%	6.2%	7.7%
55%	-2.0%	-0.5%	0.90%	2.3%	3.8%
50%	-5.9%	-4.4%	-3.0%	-1.6%	-0.1%

	Evote	Vote	2012Party ID			2015 Party ID		
Total	538	129,106	40.5%	35.2%	24.2%	36.0%	25.0%	39.0%
	Evote	Vote	Dem	Rep	Ind	Dem	Rep	Ind
AK	3	300	12.8%	26.7%	60.5%	11.4%	19.0%	69.7%
AL	9	2,074	35.0%	49.0%	16.0%	31.1%	34.8%	34.1%
AR	6	1,069	37.0%	44.0%	19.0%	32.9%	31.2%	35.9%
AZ	11	2,280	28.9%	34.4%	36.7%	25.7%	24.4%	49.9%
CA	55	13,039	43.3%	28.1%	28.6%	38.4%	19.9%	41.6%
CO	9	2,570	30.9%	32.9%	36.2%	27.4%	23.4%	49.2%
CT	7	1,559	36.4%	20.8%	42.8%	32.3%	14.8%	52.9%
DC	3	294	80.0%	10.0%	10.0%	71.0%	7.1%	21.9%
DE	3	414	47.5%	28.0%	24.5%	42.2%	19.9%	37.9%
FL	29	8,490	38.8%	35.0%	26.2%	34.5%	24.8%	40.7%
GA	16	3,900	39.0%	43.0%	18.0%	34.6%	30.5%	34.8%
HI	4	435	49.0%	35.0%	16.0%	43.5%	24.8%	31.6%
IA	6	1,582	31.1%	32.0%	36.9%	27.6%	22.7%	49.7%
ID	4	657	27.0%	52.0%	21.0%	24.0%	36.9%	39.1%
IL	20	5,244	47.0%	35.0%	18.0%	41.7%	24.8%	33.4%
IN	11	2,625	37.0%	44.0%	19.0%	32.9%	31.2%	35.9%
KS	6	1,160	24.7%	44.1%	31.2%	21.9%	31.3%	46.8%
KY	8	1,797	53.4%	38.8%	7.8%	47.4%	27.5%	25.0%
LA	8	1,994	27.1%	27.7%	45.2%	24.1%	19.7%	56.3%
MA	11	3,168	35.3%	10.9%	53.8%	31.3%	7.7%	60.9%
MD	10	2,707	54.9%	25.7%	19.4%	48.7%	18.2%	33.0%

	Evote	Vote	Dem	Rep	Ind	Dem	Rep	Ind
ME	4	713	31.9%	27.1%	41.0%	28.3%	19.2%	52.4%
MI	16	4,740	44.0%	37.0%	19.0%	39.1%	26.3%	34.7%
MN	10	2,937	44.0%	39.0%	17.0%	39.1%	27.7%	33.2%
MO	10	2,757	39.0%	44.0%	17.0%	34.6%	31.2%	34.1%
MS	6	1,286	38.0%	46.0%	16.0%	33.7%	32.7%	33.6%
MT	3	484	33.0%	51.0%	16.0%	29.3%	36.2%	34.5%
NC	15	4,505	41.7%	30.4%	27.9%	37.0%	21.6%	41.4%
ND	3	323	36.0%	47.0%	17.0%	32.0%	33.4%	34.7%
NE	5	794	30.9%	48.3%	20.8%	27.4%	34.3%	38.3%
NH	4	711	27.2%	30.1%	42.7%	24.2%	21.4%	54.5%
NJ	14	3,646	32.7%	19.7%	47.6%	29.0%	14.0%	57.0%
NM	5	784	46.6%	31.2%	22.2%	41.4%	22.1%	36.5%
NV	6	1,015	39.7%	34.6%	25.7%	35.3%	24.6%	40.2%
NY	29	7,062	49.4%	23.9%	26.7%	43.9%	17.0%	39.2%
OH	18	5,581	41.0%	42.0%	17.0%	36.4%	29.8%	33.8%
OK	7	1,335	43.7%	43.6%	12.7%	38.8%	31.0%	30.2%

	Evote	Vote	Dem	Rep	Ind	Dem	Rep	Ind
OR	7	1,789	37.8%	29.9%	32.3%	33.6%	21.2%	45.2%
PA	20	5,754	49.5%	36.7%	13.8%	44.0%	26.1%	30.0%
RI	4	446	41.5%	10.9%	47.6%	36.8%	7.7%	55.4%
SC	9	1,964	39.0%	44.0%	17.0%	34.6%	31.2%	34.1%
SD	3	364	33.8%	46.2%	20.0%	30.0%	32.8%	37.2%
TN	11	2,459	35.0%	47.0%	18.0%	31.1%	33.4%	35.6%
TX	38	7,994	37.0%	41.0%	22.0%	32.9%	29.1%	38.0%
UT	6	1,020	26.0%	59.0%	15.0%	23.1%	41.9%	35.0%
VA	13	3,854	40.0%	42.0%	18.0%	35.5%	29.8%	34.7%
VT	3	299	47.0%	31.0%	22.0%	41.7%	22.0%	36.3%
WA	12	3,141	45.0%	45.0%	10.0%	40.0%	31.9%	28.1%
WI	10	3,071	43.0%	41.0%	16.0%	38.2%	29.1%	32.7%
WV	5	671	49.4%	28.9%	21.7%	43.9%	20.5%	35.6%
WY	3	249	19.8%	66.7%	13.5%	17.6%	47.3%	35.1%

Vote shares...........................Electoral Vote

......	Stein	Clinton	Trump	Johnson	Stein	Clinton	Trump	Johnson
Total	29.5%	29.0%	25.2%	16.4%	231	196	111	0
AK	32.8%	24.1%	24.3%	18.9%	3	0	0	0
AL	26.3%	25.8%	31.0%	16.9%	0	0	9	0
AR	27.4%	27.0%	28.9%	16.7%	0	0	6	0
AZ	30.2%	26.5%	25.9%	17.4%	11	0	0	0
CA	31.1%	30.6%	22.1%	16.2%	55	0	0	0
CT	33.2%	30.1%	19.9%	16.8%	7	0	0	0
DC	34.0%	41.3%	11.8%	12.9%	0	3	0	0
DE	30.9%	31.6%	21.7%	15.8%	0	3	0	0
FL	29.6%	28.6%	25.2%	16.6%	29	0	0	0
HI	29.1%	30.9%	24.3%	15.6%	0	4	0	0
IA	30.7%	27.4%	24.7%	17.2%	6	0	0	0
ID	25.9%	23.6%	32.9%	17.6%	0	0	4	0
IL	29.2%	30.5%	24.5%	15.8%	0	20	0	0
KS	27.9%	24.2%	30.0%	17.8%	0	0	6	0
KY	28.0%	31.3%	25.4%	15.3%	0	8	0	0
LA	31.9%	27.1%	23.4%	17.6%	8	0	0	0
MA	35.7%	31.3%	16.1%	16.9%	11	0	0	0
ME	31.9%	28.2%	22.7%	17.2%	4	0	0	0
MI	28.9%	29.5%	25.5%	16.1%	0	16	0	0
MN	28.4%	29.2%	26.3%	16.1%	0	10	0	0
MO	27.3%	27.4%	28.7%	16.5%	0	0	10	0
MS	26.9%	26.9%	29.6%	16.6%	0	0	6	0

......	Stein	Clinton	Trump	Johnson	Stein	Clinton	Trump	Johnson
MT	25.9%	25.1%	32.0%	17.1%	0	0	3	0
NC	30.6%	29.9%	23.2%	16.3%	15	0	0	0
ND	26.7%	26.3%	30.2%	16.8%	0	0	3	0
NE	26.6%	25.0%	31.1%	17.3%	0	0	5	0
NH	31.3%	26.8%	24.3%	17.6%	4	0	0	0
NJ	33.7%	29.5%	19.8%	17.1%	14	0	0	0
NM	30.2%	30.9%	23.0%	15.9%	0	5	0	0
NV	29.6%	28.9%	25.0%	16.5%	6	0	0	0
NY	31.9%	32.6%	19.9%	15.6%	0	29	0	0
OH	27.7%	28.1%	27.8%	16.4%	0	18	0	0
OK	27.2%	28.5%	28.1%	16.1%	0	7	0	0
OR	30.9%	29.1%	23.3%	16.6%	7	0	0	0
PA	28.7%	30.8%	24.9%	15.6%	0	20	0	0
RI	35.4%	32.7%	15.6%	16.3%	4	0	0	0
SD	27.0%	25.9%	30.0%	17.0%	0	0	3	0
TN	26.8%	26.1%	30.2%	16.9%	0	0	11	0
TX	28.2%	27.4%	27.7%	16.7%	38	0	0	0
UT	24.2%	22.4%	35.7%	17.7%	0	0	6	0
VA	27.8%	27.9%	27.8%	16.4%	0	13	0	0
VT	30.2%	31.0%	22.9%	15.8%	0	3	0	0
WA	26.8%	28.6%	28.6%	16.0%	0	12	0	0
WI	27.9%	28.7%	27.2%	16.2%	0	10	0	0
WV	30.6%	31.9%	21.9%	15.6%	0	5	0	0
WY	22.5%	19.9%	39.3%	18.2%	0	0	3	0

10. 2014 Governor Elections

The basic premise is that Republican increase in cumulative precinct vote shares is counter-intuitive since the Democrats do much better in urban and suburban counties than in rural areas where the GOP is dominant. Precincts in Urban areas contain more voters than rural areas.

Since the GOP gains share in Democratic locations in virtually all of the competitive elections analyzed, it is highly suggestive evidence that Democratic precincts are where the majority of votes are stolen. In competitive elections, the correlation between county/precinct vote-size and the change in Democratic vote share is negative; Democrats lose share as county/precinct size increase. On the other hand, in non-competitive races, the Statistical correlation is close to zero; there is virtually no relationship. The numerical evidence in each election is clear.

The focus is on the largest counties (approximately 64% of the total vote). The True Vote is estimated as the sum of the cumulative precinct votes in the largest counties at the 10% mark and the recorded votes in other counties. We compare the cumulative vote shares of the counties at the 10% mark to the final result. The Democrats have an average 52.5% True Vote compared to their 46.9% recorded vote. We would normally expect little or no divergence in the trend lines from the 10% mark. But the sharp divergence favoring the GOP from the 10% mark to the final is counter intuitive and violates the Law of Large Numbers (LLN).

Cumulative vote shares

10% CVS: Dem 52.0-45.0% to Final: Rep 50.0-46.9%

Final	Total	Dem	Rep	Other	Dem	Rep
Top	10,745,395	5,446,214	5,004,052	298,006	50.7%	46.6%
Other	5,981,873	2,398,401	3,366,396	212,110	40.1%	56.3%
Total	16,727,268	7,844,616	8,370,447	510,116	46.9%	50.0%
KY	974,344	426,947	511,719	35,678	43.8%	52.5%
IL	3,626,504	1,681,343	1,823,627	121,534	46.4%	50.3%
FL	5,889,897	2,801,112	2,865,343	223,356	47.6%	48.6%
WI	2,382,055	1,112,260	1,242,413	27,383	46.7%	52.2%
MD *	1,733,177	818,890	884,400	29,887	47.2%	51.0%
MA	2,120,795	1,004,408	1,044,573	71,814	47.4%	49.3%

10% CVS	Dem	Rep	Other	Dem	Rep	Other
Top	6,276,680	4,175,896	291,455	58.4%	38.9%	2.7%
Other	2,415,852	3,354,794	212,201	40.4%	56.1%	3.5%
Total	8,692,532	7,530,690	503,656	52.0%	45.0%	3.0%
KY	482,300	452,096	40,922	49.5%	46.4%	4.2%
IL	1,969,548	1,544,436	113,017	54.4%	42.5%	3.1%
FL	3,008,216	2,659,288	222,393	51.1%	45.1%	3.8%
WI	1,194,970	1,159,878	25,844	50.2%	48.7%	1.1%
MD	903,589	777,012	29,069	52.9%	45.4%	1.7%
MA	1,187,638	861,362	71,795	56.0%	40.6%	3.4%

2014 WI Governor Voter True Vote Model

The Cumulative Vote Share (CVS) analysis tracks cumulative vote shares for each county based on increasing unit/ward voting size. The odd pattern of increasing Walker vote shares in large Democratic counties was similar to the 2012 WI recall. This counter-intuitive trend is highly indicative of fraud.

Assuming an equal 77% turnout of 2012 Obama and Romney voters (proportional to the 2012 recorded vote), Burke won the True Vote by 51.6-47.3%. She lost the official vote to Walker by 52.2-46.7%. This was close to the Cumulative Vote Share result which had her winning with 50.2%.

2012	Record	Votes	Alive	Return	Votes		Pct	Burke	Walker	Other	Turnout
Obama	52.8%	1,621	1,588	1,112	1,112		46.7%	91.0%	8.0%	1.0%	70%
Romney	45.9%	1,411	1,383	968	968		40.6%	7.0%	93.0%	0.0%	70%
Other	1.3%	39	39	27	27		1.1%	48.0%	48.0%	4.0%	70%
Did Not Vote		-	-		275		11.6%	50.0%	45.5%	4.5%	
											Margin
	Total	3,071	3,010	2,107	2,382	Share		51.6%	47.3%	1.0%	4.3%
					77.6%	Votes		1,230	1,127	25	103
						Recorded	46.7%	52.2%	1.1%		-5.5%
						Vote	1,112	1,242	27		-130
						CVS-10%	50.2%	48.7%	1.1%		1.5%
						Vote	1,195	1,160	27		35

2014 WI Governor Voter Turnout Model

Registered	3005		Split	Reg	Turnout	Votes		Burke	Walker	Other
Votes	2382	Dem	43.0%	1,292	79.3%	1,024		95%	4%	1%
Other	1.15%	Rep	41.0%	1,232	79.3%	977		7%	92%	1%
Turnout	79.3%	Ind	16.0%	481	79.3%	381		49%	49%	2%
		Total	100.0%	3,005	79.3%	2382		51.6%	47.3%	1.2%

	Burke		Burke	% Dem		
% Rep	87.0%	89.0%	91.0%	93.0%	95.0%	
Burke						
9.0%	48.9%	49.8%	50.7%	51.5%	52.4%	
7.0%	48.1%	49.0%	49.8%	50.7%	51.6%	
5.0%	47.3%	48.2%	49.0%	49.9%	50.7%	
Margin (000)						
9.0%	-23	18	59	100	141	
7.0%	-62	-21	20	61	102	
5.0%	-101	-60	-19	22	63	

2014 Wisconsin Governor Election: Milwaukee County

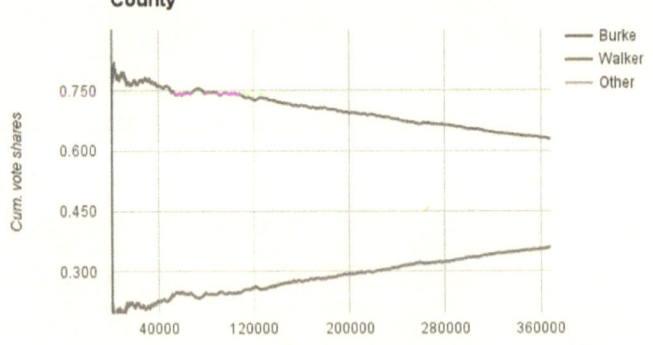

Cumulative Votes - smallest to largest precincts

2014 Florida True Vote Model

2012	Recorded	Votes	Alive	Return	Votes	Pct	Crist	Scott	Other	Turnout
Obama	49.9%	4,198	4,114	2,468	2,468	41.55%	91.0%	5.0%	4.0%	60%
Romney	49.0%	4,124	4,042	2,425	2,425	40.82%	9.0%	88.9%	4.0%	60%
Other	1.0%	88	86	52	52	0.87%	46.0%	46.0%	8.0%	60%
DNV		-	-		996	16.76%	47.9%	44.1%	8.0%	
										Margin
TOTAL		8,410	8,242	4,945	5,941	Share	49.9%	45.4%	4.7%	4.5%
						Votes	2,965	2,696	280	269
						Recorded	47.1%	48.2%	4.7%	-1.1%
						Vote	2,798	2,864	279	-65
						CVS	51.1%	45.1%	3.8%	5.9%
						Vote	3,034	2,682	224	352

t   Crist share of returning Obama voters

Share of Romney	87%	89%	91%	93%	95%
		Crist Vote Share			
11.0%	49.1%	49.9%	50.7%	51.6%	52.4%
10.0%	48.7%	49.5%	50.3%	51.2%	52.0%
9.0%	48.3%	49.1%	49.9%	50.7%	51.6%
8.0%	47.8%	48.7%	49.5%	50.3%	51.2%
7.0%	47.4%	48.3%	49.1%	49.9%	50.8%
			Margin (000)		
11.0%	168.9	267.6	366.3	465.1	563.8
10.0%	120.4	219.1	317.8	416.6	515.3
9.0%	71.9	170.6	269.3	368.1	466.8
8.0%	23.4	122.1	220.8	319.6	418.3
7.0%	-25.1	73.6	172.3	271.1	369.8

Pct	Crist	Scott	Other
38.8%	81.3%	14.7%	4.0%
35.0%	10.0%	88.0%	2.0%
26.2%	46.0%	45.0%	9.0%
100%	**47.1%**	**48.3%**	**4.6%**
5,941	**2,798.2**	**2,868.9**	**273.9**

	Pct	Crist	Scott	Other
Dem	38.8%	88.6%	8.4%	3%
Rep	35.0%	10%	88%	2%
Other	26.2%	46%	45%	9%
Share	**100%**	**49.9%**	**45.4%**	**4.7%**
Vote	**5,941**	**2,798**	**2,697**	**279**

2014 Illinois Governor True Vote Model

Rauner won by 50.2-46.3%. But Quinn won the CVS 55.2-41.8% and the TVM by 53.8-42.8%.

County	Quinn	Raunier	Grimm	Quinn	Raunier	Grimm	Change
Top 15	1695	1030	73	61.5%	35.9%	2.6%	10.5%
Other 87	252	535	40	33.5%	64.6%	1.9%	3.1%
Total	**1,947**	**1,565**	**114**	**55.2%**	**41.8%**	**3.1%**	**8.8%**

VTM	Split	Reg	Turnout	Votes	Quinn	Rauner	Grimm			
Dem	47.0%	2,687	60.0%	1,612	91%	7%	2%			
Rep	35.0%	2,001	68.0%	1,361	7%	91%	2%			
Ind	18.0%	1,029	63.4%	653	40%	53%	7%			
Total	**100%**	**5,716**	**63.4%**	**3626**	**50.3%**	**46.8%**	**2.9%**			
Obama	57.6%	3,019	2,959	1,775	1,775	49.0%	90.0%	8.0%	2.0%	60%
Romney	40.7%	2,135	2,092	1,255	1,255	34.6%	7.0%	91.0%	2.0%	60%
Other	1.7%	89	88	53	53	1.5%	43.5%	43.5%	13.0%	60%
DNV (new)		-	-		543	15.0%	45.0%	45.0%	10.0%	
Total		**5,244**	**5,139**	**3,083**	**3,626**	**True Share**	**53.8%**	**42.8%**	**3.4%**	**11.0%**
					69.1%	**Vote (000)**	**1,952**	**1,552**	**122**	**400**

2014 Massachusetts Governor True Vote Model

Baker (R) won by 48.5-46.6%.

Registered Democrats far outnumbered Republicans (35-10%).

Coakley won by 55.7-39.5% assuming just 60% Democratic turnout vs. 86% Republican and an equal 47% split of Independents. She won the CVS by 56.0-40.6% and the TVM by 55.6-39.5%, a triple confirmation.

	Split	Reg	Turnout	Votes	Coakley	Baker	Other
Dem	35.3%	1,147	60.0%	688	91%	5%	4%
Rep	10.9%	354	86.0%	304	9%	87%	4%
Ind	53.8%	1,749	66.1%	1,156	47%	47%	6%
Total	**100.0%**	**3,250**	**66.1%**	**2149**	**55.7%**	**39.4%**	**4.9%**

Maryland

Hogan (R) won by 51.03-47.25%, but Brown won the adj. CVS 50.65-47.67%.

Note the disparity between Election Day vs. early, absentee and provisional voting

Votes	Total	Brown	Share	Hogan	Share	Other	Share
Early	305,594	164,219	53.74%	136,781	44.76%	4,594	1.50%
Election Day	1,342,837	608,476	45.31%	710,854	52.94%	23,507	1.75%
Abs/prov	84,746	46,195	54.51%	36,765	43.38%	1,786	2.11%
Recorded	**1,733,177**	**818,890**	**47.25%**	**884,400**	**51.03%**	**29,887**	**1.72%**
Early/abs/prov	390,340	210,414	53.91%	173,546	44.46%	6,380	1.63%
CVS @ 10%	1,342,837	667,390	49.70%	652,619	48.60%	22,828	1.70%
Adj. Total	**1,733,177**	**877,804**	**50.65%**	**826,165**	**47.67%**	**29,208**	**1.69%**

2014 Michigan Governor True Vote Model

Snyder won by 51.0-46.8%. To match the recorded vote, Snyder needed 19% of returning Obama voters, Independents to increase from 19% (registered) to 31% (Party-ID) and win them by 64-33%. Schauer (D) won the true vote by 52.4-45.3%.

2012	Recorded	Votes	Alive	Return	Votes	Pct	Schauer	Snyder	Other	Turnout
Obama	54.1%	2,565	2,514	1,508	1,508	48.1%	91.0%	7.0%	2.0%	60%
Romney	44.6%	2,115	2,073	1,244	1,244	39.6%	7.0%	91.0%	2.0%	60%
Other	1.3%	60	59	35	35	1.1%	48.0%	48.0%	4.0%	60%
Did Not Vote (new)		-	-		351	11.2%	48.0%	48.0%	4.0%	
										Margin
TOTAL		4,740	4,645	2,787	3,138	Share	52.4%	45.3%	2.2%	7.1%
						66.2%	Vote	1,645	1,422	70	223

Party-ID	Pct	Schauer	Snyder	Other
Democrat	39%	88.4%	9.6%	2%
Republican	30%	7%	91.0%	2%
Other	31%	33%	64.0%	3%
Share	100%	46.8%	50.9%	2.3%
Vote		1,469	1,597	72

2014 Vermont Governor True Vote Model

Shumlin (D) won a squeaker 46.4-45.3%. But it should not have been so close.

Registered Democrats led Republicans by 47-31%.

Shumlin won the True Vote by 54-40%

Model Assumptions

1. Shumlin has 86% of returning Obama voters and 4% of Romney voters.

2. Equal 60% turnout

3. Equal 42% share of Independents.

2012	Recorded	Votes	Alive	Return	Votes	Pct	Shumlin	Milne	Other	Turnout
Obama	66.1%	198	194	107	107	54.9%	86.0%	11.0%	3.0%	55%
Romney	31.0%	93	91	59	59	30.4%	4.0%	93.0%	3.0%	65%
Other	2.9%	9	8	6	6	2.8%	40.0%	40.0%	20.0%	65%
DNV (new)		-	-		23	11.8%	40.0%	40.0%	20.0%	
										Margin
TOTAL		299	293	171	194	Share 54.3%	40.2%	5.5%	14.1%	
						Vote 105	78	11	27	

Registration

	Split	Voters	Turnout	Votes	Shumlin	Milne	Other
Dem	47.0%	152	59.9%	91	90.0%	5.0%	5.0%
Rep	31.0%	100	59.9%	60	6.0%	89.0%	5.0%
Ind	22.0%	71	59.9%	43	42.0%	42.0%	16.0%
		324	59.9%	194	53.4%	39.2%	7.4%

Governor 2012 Elections: Recorded vote closely matched the True Vote

CO	Recorded	Votes	Alive	Return	Votes	Pct	Hickenlooper	Beauprez	Other	Turnout
Obama	51.5%	1,324	1,297	908	908	45.6%	90.0%	5.0%	5.0%	70%
Romney	46.1%	1,186	1,162	814	814	40.8%	7.4%	87.6%	5.0%	70%
Other	2.4%	61	60	42	42	2.1%	48.5%	48.5%	3.0%	70%
DNV		-	-		229	11.5%	49.0%	48.0%	3.0%	
TOTAL		2,571	2,520	1,764	1,993	Share	50.7%	44.6%	4.7%	6.1%
						77.5%	Vote 1,010	889	94	121

OR	Recorded	Votes	Alive	Return	Votes	Pct	Kitzhaber	Richardson	Other	Turnout
Obama	54.2%	970	950	713	713	48.5%	87.0%	8.0%	5.0%	75%
Romney	42.2%	755	740	555	555	37.8%	5.0%	90.0%	5.0%	75%
Other	3.6%	64	63	47	47	3.2%	50.0%	45.0%	5.0%	75%
DNV		-	-		154	10.5%	44.0%	46.0%	10.0%	
TOTAL		1,789	1,753	1,315	1,469	Share	50.3%	44.2%	5.5%	6.2%
						Vote	739	649	81	91

PA	Recorded	Votes	Alive	Return	Votes	Pct	Wolf	Corbett	Turnout
Obama	52.0%	2,992	2,932	1,613	1,613	46.5%	92.0%	8.0%	55%
Romney	46.6%	2,681	2,628	1,445	1,445	41.7%	16.0%	84.0%	55%
Other	1.4%	81	79	43	43	1.3%	55.0%	45.0%	55%
DNV		-	-		369	10.6%	55.0%	45.0%	
TOTAL		5,754	5,639	3,101	3,470	Share	56.0%	44.0%	11.9%

References

https://richardcharnin.wordpress.com/category/2016-election/

Election Fraud 2016 https://electionfraud2016.wordpress.com/

Bev Harris http://blackboxvoting.org/fraction-magic-1/

http://marionumber1.blogspot.com/2016/09/election-fraud-part-4-clinton-shift.html

Institute for American Democracy and Election Integrity

http://thefreethoughtproject.com/election-fraud-rico-lawsuit-alleging-widespread-e-vote-rigging-dnc-primaries-derail-clinton-nomination/#5XdQHFWIYPOLXpsa.99

Stanford University

http://alexanderhiggins.com/stanford-berkley-study-1-77-billion-chance-hillary-won-primary-without-widespread-election-fraud/

Electoral Justice USA http://electionjustice.net/democracy-lost-a-report-on-the-fatally-flawed-2016-democratic-primaries-table-of-contents/

Just Doing the Math

http://www.democracyintegrity.org/ElectoralFraud/just-doing-the-math.html

Doug Johnson Hatlem

http://www.counterpunch.org/2016/05/11/hillary-clinton-versus-bernie-sanders-in-depth-report-on-exit-polling-and-election-fraud-allegations/

John Laurits https://johnlaurits.com/2016/08/22/why-sanders-supporters-are-mad-why-everyone-else-should-be-too/

Truth seekers

Tim Robbins http://thehill.com/blogs/ballot-box/presidential-races/277537-actor-tim-robbins-blames-voter-fraud-for-sanders-losses

http://www.huffingtonpost.com/tim-robbins/fix-our-election-system_b_9847102.html

Lee Camp http://leecamp.net/my-response-to-being-attacked-by-josh-holland-in-raw-story-concerning-exitpollgate/

http://leecamp.net/category/redacted-tonight/

Beth Clarkson http://showmethevotes.org/2016/06/10/the-theater-is-on-fire/

Bob Fitrakis http://freepress.org/article/professor-fitrakis-flunks-nations-joshua-holland-exit-polls

Bob Fitrakis http://freepress.org/article/2016-election-already-being-stripped-flipped

Nina Illingworth
http://www.ninaillingworth.com/2016/05/07/recommended-reading-election-fraud-mega-edition/

Debbie Lusignan (Sane Progressive)
https://electionfraud2016.wordpress.com/2016/03/03/sane-progressive-sanders-needs-to-address-voter-fraud-now/

https://www.facebook.com/saneprogressive/

Spencer Gundert https://medium.com/@spencergundert/hillary-clinton-and-electoral-fraud-992ad9e080f6#.4wdi30pje

Interviews

Thom Hartmann:
https://www.youtube.com/watch?v=9oJR5ZDtxGg

Jim Fetzer: https://www.youtube.com/watch?v=7mTvgfsEnZg

Lee Camp: https://www.youtube.com/watch?v=R6x8Z4NLUAA

Sane Progressive:
https://www.youtube.com/watch?v=pyC7lF8G1GA

Sane Progressive:
https://www.youtube.com/watch?v=czaj6EH8bSl

Nicolas Knolin:
https://www.youtube.com/watch?v=lUwxduQchR4

NY BOE:
https://www.youtube.com/watch?v=AFjxYLsFDIQ&sns=fb

PDA: https://www.youtube.com/watch?v=mThZiN5yoY8

Naysayers

Joshua Holland http://www.rawstory.com/2016/04/on-tim-robbins-election-fraud-and-how-nonsense-spreads-around-the-internet/

Joshua Holland https://www.thenation.com/article/reminder-exit-poll-conspiracy-theories-are-totally-baseless/

Philip Bump https://www.washingtonpost.com/news/the-fix/wp/2016/04/25/you-need-to-chill-out-tim-robbins/

Nate Cohn http://www.nytimes.com/2016/06/28/upshot/exit-polls-and-why-the-primary-was-not-stolen-from-bernie-sanders.html?_r=0

Chris Mathews http://fortune.com/2016/08/04/trump-election-rigged/

Polls
*http://www.realclearpolitics.com/epolls/2016/president/us/gener
al election trump vs clinton vs johnson vs stein-5952.html*

http://www.ipsos-na.com/news-polls/pressrelease.aspx?id=7349

http://www.gallup.com/poll/15370/party-affiliation.aspx

Historical Election Fraud posts

Prof. Michael Keefe: The Strange Death of American
Democracy: Endgame in Ohio

Prof. Michael Keefer: Footprints of Electoral Fraud

Prof. Michael Keefer: Election Fraud in America

Prof. Keefer: Evidence of Fraud in the 2004 U.S. Presidential
Election: A Reader

Prof. Michael Keefer: 2006 US Midterms: Another Stolen
Election?

Bob Fitrakis: Missing Votes in Ohio 2006 Midterms

Bob Fitrakis: new evidence on the 2004 Ohio stolen election

Bob Fitrakis: Court filing reveals 2004 Ohio election was hacked

Greg Palast: Kerry Won

Greg Palast: Recipe for a Cooked Election

Jonathan Simon, Election Defense Alliance: Landslide Denied

Thom Hartmann: Evidence Mounts that the Vote May Have Been Hacked

Professor Steven F. Freeman: The Unexplained Exit Poll Discrepancy

Prof. John Allen Paulos: Final Tallies – Exit Polls: A Statistical Mystery

Robert Koehler: Silent Scream of The Numbers

Robert F. Kennedy Jr: Was the 2004 Election Stolen?

Mark Crispin Miller: None Dare Call It Stolen

Mark Crispin Miller: Some Might Call it Treason – An Open Letter to Salon

Ernest Partridge: Bush Wins Florida – NOT

Michael Collins: The Urban Legend

Sheila Parks: 2011 Wisconsin Uprising: The New Florida and Ohio?

Richard Charnin

Avoiding Election Fraud: Political Scientists, Academics and the Media

Footprints of Election Fraud: 1988-2008 State Exit Poll Discrepancies

Monte Carlo Simulation: 2004 Presidential Pre-election and Exit Polls

An Electoral Vote Forecasting: Simulation or Meta-analysis not required

The unadjusted 2004 National Exit Poll: closing the book on "False Recall"

True Vote Graphics

Unadjusted Exit Poll Probability Analysis Links

Election Fraud: Uncertainty, Logic and Probability

A Model for Estimating Presidential Election Day Fraud

2000-2012: Monte Carlo Electoral Vote Simulation

2004: Simple Arithmetic Proof that Bush Stole the election

2004: The "Game" Debate

Why did the Networks Cancel Exit Polls in 19 States?

2000 Unadjusted Exit Polls: Gore won by 51-45% (5-7 million votes)

2004: True Vote Model Sensitivity Analysis: Kerry Landslide

A Conversation about the 2004 Election

Simple Numerical Proof of 2004 Election Fraud

Returning 2000 and New Voters: Proof that Kerry Won

Online Book: Confirmation of a Kerry Landslide

2008: To believe Obama by just 9.5 million-votes

Proof that Obama won by much more than 9.5 million votes

2008 Unadjusted Exit Polls Confirm the True Vote Model

1988-2008 State Uncounted Votes and Exit Poll Analysis

The True Vote Model: A Mathematical Formulation

True Vote Model: Probability Sensitivity Analysis

An Introduction to the True Vote Model

Election Fraud Quiz

Election Fraud Quiz II

About the author

Richard Charnin graduated from Queens College (NY) in 1965 with a BA in Mathematics. He was hired as a numerical control engineer/programmer by Grumman Aerospace Corporation, a major defense/aerospace manufacturer which built the Lunar Module, commercial aircraft and carrier-based fighters.

He obtained an MS in Applied Mathematics from Adelphi University and an MS in Operations Research from the Polytechnic Institute of NY.

In 1976, he was hired as a manager/developer of corporate finance quantitative applications for White Weld & Co, a Wall Street investment bank that was acquired by Merrill Lynch in 1978.

In 1986, Charnin became an independent software developer, specializing in quantitative applications development for major domestic and foreign financial institutions and industrial corporations.

In 2004 he posted presidential election projections based on state and national pre-election polls. The final forecast matched the unadjusted exit polls which Kerry won by 51-47%, a 6 million vote margin.

In 2008, Charnin exactly forecast Obama's recorded vote (365 EV, 53% share). His True Vote Model (TVM) indicated that Obama had 420 EV and a 58% share, exactly matching the unadjusted exit polls.

In 2012, he exactly forecast Obama's recorded vote (332 EV, 51%). The TVM indicated that Obama had 391 EV and 55%. The National Election Pool decided not to exit poll in 19 states.

Charnin determined that the 1988-2008 presidential exit polls proved systemic Election Fraud. The Democrats won the unadjusted state and national exit polls by 52-42%. But their recorded vote margin was 48-46%. Of the 274 state exit polls, 135 exceeded the margin of error (131 shifted to the Republicans in the recorded vote).

In the 2016 Democratic primaries, Sander's unadjusted exit poll share exceeded his recorded vote share by more than the margin of error in 11 of 26 primaries – a 1 in 77 billion probability. The primaries were stolen from Sanders by the hacking and stripping of voter registration rolls and flipping of votes on electronic voting machines.

www.ingramcontent.com/pod-product-compliance
Lightning Source LLC
Chambersburg PA
CBHW030440290526
45786CB00001B/371